So You Want to Retire

*Learning From Others'
Retirement Planning Mistakes*

By: Arthur S. Montgomery

Eloquent Books

Eloquent Books
An imprint of Strategic Book Group
P.O. Box 333
Durham CT 06422
www.StrategicBookGroup.com

ISBN 978-1-60860-935-2

Printed in the United States of America

Table of Contents

Acknowledgements

I would first like to acknowledge my parents, who taught me that anything is possible no matter what other people say to you.

My father taught me how to read the financial section of the newspaper when I was in eighth grade; this gave me the desire to become a financial advisor (that is, if I couldn't be a fighter pilot). This back-up plan worked out well, because by the age of fifteen I was too tall to become a fighter pilot. This made becoming a financial advisor the perfect choice; there is no height limit for financial advisors.

My mother helped pay for my first two years of college, and encouraged and supported me through all of my activities and endeavors. She drove thirty miles each day, for six years, to pick me up from basketball and track practice. She drove to most of my games and track meets, sitting in the stands and knitting sweaters.

My sister, Rose, read this book, gave me critical feedback on my grammatical errors, and helped me make the necessary corrections.

My long-time friend, canoeing, fishing, and hunting buddy, Jerry Castillon, was the first one to read this book once it was finished. His job was to see if it was worth reading. He said it was.

Introduction

The information in this book has been compiled from my nineteen years (and counting) as a financial adviser, working with retirees and pre-retirees. My advice stems from the many clients I have had the privilege to work with, and the experiences they have shared with me. In my examples I will keep the particular details as general as possible. Hopefully this will allow you, the reader, to relate to the situation. Many of the stories I tell will be a compilation of several clients with very similar circumstances. Some of the stories are events that happened to friends or clients of fellow brokers or advisors. I want to provide you with enough information so you can learn from other's experiences and mistakes. I don't want to get bogged down in minute details, and I definitely do not want someone who reads this book to say, "I know who he is talking about."

Any specific data or statistics given in this book will have the source and rationale included with the example. Anybody can make up statistics to prove a point; I want you to see a credible source for this information. The sources I use to provide this information are from outlets I believe to be reliable, but I do not guarantee their accuracy.

I wanted to write this book because I see how many people are lost when it comes to planning their retirement. Trying to get pertinent information on how to plan your retirement can be like trying to take a sip of water from a fire hose. If I can help you plan a long and happy retirement, then I have accomplished my goal.

In this book, I have tried to provide you with the basic information on how to plan and prepare for retirement. The hard stuff, such as determining a budget or estimating income, you will have to do yourself. Someone once observed that the average American spends more time picking out clothes than they do planning how they will spend their retirement years.

The "How To" retirement books I have read were either too technical or were based on someone trying to sell something. They didn't tell the reader how to plan for retirement beyond the financial needs. I wanted to include ways to stay healthy, mentally sharp, and active in retirement. I also want to give you a basic understanding of when might be a good time to retire.

To avoid having good information buried in a lot of theory and a pile of statistics, I have kept the topics as straightforward as I can. Many books have been written about investing and investment theories, attempting to define how you should invest your money once you retire. I am not going to spend a lot of time talking about how you should invest your money; how to invest your money would be an entire book all to itself. What I will discuss, regarding investments, are the things that apply to most people who are planning their retirement.

Although I have attempted to cover all of the bases regarding retirement planning, a majority of this book deals with the financial aspects of the retirement planning process. This is for a couple of different reasons: One, I am in the financial services industry and this is the area I am most knowledgeable about; Two, in the numerous studies I have read and surveys I have seen, financial issues tend to be one of the leading reasons for discontent during the retirement years.

This being said, people who focus solely on money tend to be among the most miserable people I have talked with. P.T. Barnum was quoted as saying, "Money makes an excellent servant but a terrible master." Having viewed this first hand, I believe this to be a very accurate statement.

Most of my clients and friends who are retired and happy have several things in common. In my writing, I mention these and go into some detail as to enable you to have a guideline on some of the activities to participate in or some of the traps to avoid.

The first part of this book is a "How To" plan for your retirement years that will help you get the maximum benefit from your health and resources.

The second part of this book consists of retirement resources, investment information, and a glossary of definitions. These are frequently used words and phrases that many people have heard, but don't know quite what they mean. I hope you enjoy my book.

The examples in this book are all hypothetical in nature and do not depict an investment in any particular product. They also do not take into account the effect of dividends received or the effect that taxes may have on withdrawals. If any of these examples pertain to your specific situation and you have questions about the effect of taxes, please consult a professional tax advisor.

CHAPTER 1
Retirement Basics

"Retirement has been a discovery of beauty for me. I never had the time before to notice the beauty of my grandkids, my wife, the tree outside my very own front door. And, the beauty of time itself."
—Hartman Jule

Retirement is a lot like life; you have decisions to make and each decision has a consequence. People are often asking me, "How much money do I need to have saved before I can retire?" And, "What is the best age for me to retire?"

It will all depend on what is most important to you. Do you want to have more income in retirement, or do you want to spend more years being retired?

No matter what your retirement plans may be, decide for yourself what your priorities are and build your retirement around them.

Before you decide to retire, if you are married, talk it over with your spouse. A surprise like the announcement that you have just retired might send them over the edge. And, if you expect to spend the rest of your life with them and have many happy years together, surprising them with that announcement is not a good way to start. Yes, I have had a client or two retire without giving their spouse any warning.

Think of retirement like a long road trip across the country. Many people want to plan this trip, but they never get around to it. When the time comes, they just take off driving without doing much planning. Others will make a budget to see what they can afford, plan a route so they can visit places of interest along the way, and have their car inspected to make sure there are no major problems with it before they start. A few people will have the money to stay at the Four Seasons or the Ritz Carlton on their journey. Some will want to stay at the expensive hotels but are not be able to afford such extravagances. Most people are happy staying at a safe, clean, comfortable place. There are also those who will stay wherever they can without much choice.

If you were to drive cross-country, what would be the first thing you would do? Would you set down and plan a date, a route, and a budget? Can you imagine driving across the country without doing any planning? Picture yourself taking a trip like this with $50 in your pocket, jumping into a 1984 Chevy Impala that you just bought for $250, and no map. Would you ever attempt such a journey? Would you discuss it with anyone else, or would you just go?

If the idea of starting a cross-country trip with little resources and almost no planning sounds ridiculous to you, consider how many people start their retirement this way.

Some people will plan and save for such a major event, but most will just take off on a "grand adventure." Considering how few people actually spend a reasonable amount of time planning for their own retirement, it appears that most people would take the "grand adventure" route. A grand adventure can be exciting and unpredictable. Do you want to pin your retirement hopes, dreams that you have worked on for so many years, on luck?

If you think the idea of not planning a trip that might take a few weeks and cost a few thousand dollars is ridiculous, how does it sound to have no reasonable plan before starting a trip that might take the next thirty years and cost over a million dollars? That is what a majority of people do; they just retire and hope for the best. And yes, there is a good chance that you will spend over $1,000,000 in retirement.

How are you planning to spend your retirement years? The fact that you are taking time to read this book puts you in the minority of people who will actually take the time to put some thought into how you want to spend the next twenty to forty years or more. Retirement is an individual thing; it is as personal as your favorite food, the colors you like, or your favorite song. This is where you decide what you want to do, how much money you want to spend, and where you want to live. No one else can make these decisions for you.

I hope you are able to accomplish everything that you have planned for, and more, when you retire. I also hope that you find the information in this book useful and worthwhile.

There is one thing certain in retirement; no two people will retire with the exact same aspirations, goals, and resources. Whether its years spent retired or activities done during retirement, everyone who retires will have a unique experience.

Because of this, there is no cookie-cutter retirement. How could there be a cookie-cutter approach to retirement planning? When it comes to your retirement, there is no cookie-cutter formula that will guarantee you the type of retirement you want.

So many of us have heard the statements that, in order to have a secure retirement we need to have sixteen times our annual salary set aside before we retire. We need to be able to make 60 to 70 percent of our working income once we retire. You should invest your age as a percentage in bonds, so if you are age sixty you have 60 percent bonds and 40 percent stocks. All of these statements are absolutely correct if you are earning $48,201, live in a house worth $213,900, will live to be 83.7 years old, retire at age sixty-four, and live in

Phelps County, 2.8 miles east of Edgar Springs, Missouri. According to the Bureau of Labor Statistics, these are the average household incomes, average home values, and the life expectancy of a sixty-five-year-old for the year of 2005. The Phelps County reference was the population center of the U.S. according to the census bureau for 2005.

The point I am trying to make is that there are no rules of thumb or guidelines that are right for you unless you are perfectly average. Very few people are average; most are either above or below average. It is the vast majority of people, the non-average people, that can benefit from an individual plan.

Don't get me wrong; I am not saying that guidelines and rules of thumb are worthless. I am just saying they cannot be universally applied to your specific circumstances. Guidelines or rules of thumb are simply a basis for a person to evaluate how well or poorly they are doing compared to the average person. If your income in retirement is going to be 60 percent to 70 percent of your working income, that might work out very well for you. I have clients who will be able to live comfortably off of 30 percent of their current income once they retire. I have other clients that will need more than their current income once they retire.

Here is a quick analogy. The yellow-diamond warning signs indicating a curve ahead, with the speed listed below, are guidelines. The speed listed is the guideline that someone has decided is the safe speed required for the average driver, in an average car, to be able to safely make it around the curve. If you are an above-average driver, and are driving a nice sports car, you could actually safely take the curve much faster than the guideline speed. On the other hand, if you are driving a 1966 Ford pickup truck with a broken leaf spring and bald tires, this recommended speed might be faster than you could safely take the curve. It all comes down to your resources, abilities, and desires.

Let's agree on this point; there is no, "one size fits all" rule of thumb to use for your retirement plan. Every person has different ideas about how to spend their retirement. This being said, how can someone who has never met you, and has no idea what you want to do when you retire, know what you need to have in order to retire? This takes some thought and planning, based on your dreams and desires.

I have people ask me how much money they need to have set aside in order to retire. The answer is simple. They have enough money to retire now, if they are willing to accept the standard of living their resources are able to provide to them. How much does it cost to be a hermit up in the woods? If you want more comfort and luxury than the hermit lifestyle, you will need to have more money set aside than someone who wants to live in a small cabin in the woods. If the small cabin in the woods sounds like the perfect retirement to you, you are probably doing just fine.

If you want to plan for "your" retirement, you will have to develop a plan to fit your unique circumstances and desired lifestyle. This is because the definition of a perfect retirement is different for every person. How you plan to spend your retirement is as individual as your taste in clothing, food, and music.

Just as there are no rules of thumb that hold true on what type of music you should listen to, there are no rules of thumb on how you should invest, the amount of money you need to earn, how you should spend your time, or the lifestyle you should have once you retire.

If there were a "one size fits all" answer I could say that when you hit age sixty-five you should spend ninety minutes a day listening to music, and it should be 40 percent classical, 20 percent soft jazz, 15 percent Broadway musicals, and 25 percent golden oldies. No blues or rock and roll; that is not appropriate for someone your age.

As Americans, we do not like to be told what we like or dislike.

We have come to appreciate our freedoms. So, why do so many of us accept these statements regarding retirement guidelines without question?

Although rules of thumb and guidelines might not always hold true for your circumstances, there are some constants in the world of finance that have not changed since the invention of money. Those are, "The more money you have the higher your chances for financial security," and, "The less money you spend, the less likely you are to run out of money."

You're probably wondering why I mention those two statements, as they are so obvious and self-explanatory. I mention them because sometimes we overlook the most obvious things. Have you ever spent time looking for a hat you were wearing, or keys that you had in your hand? Sometimes we think about so many things that we forget to think about the most obvious things.

Here is another way of saying it. The larger your savings gets, the less likely you are to run out of money before your retirement ends. The less money you spend, the less likely you are to run out of money.

So, now that you have seen the obvious, let's discuss some more obvious truths about retirement. When you work longer and retire later, you have the potential for a more financially secure retirement. This occurs for two very simple reasons.

First, the more years you spend working, the fewer years you will spend in retirement. Second, theoretically, the longer you work the more contributions you will make to social security, savings, pension, and other areas that can provide you income once you retire. Once you retire, you are trading a job where you earn money for a permanent vacation (theoretically) and are no longer working for pay.

During your retirement you stop adding money to your savings, retirement plan, social security, and pension, and start pulling money out of those places. These accounts will stop growing as fast as they did when you were working. You have gone from saving money to spending the money you have saved.

And, let's not forget the most powerful force in the universe. According to Benjamin Franklin, that force is compound interest. The longer your money is invested, the more opportunity you have for growth and the more interest you will earn. The moment you start cashing in your investment gains and stop reinvesting your interest, in order to pay for living expenses, you lessen the power of compounding.

Let's say you are thinking about retiring and you are fifty-five years old. You have $500,000 in savings. If you have paid into the Social Security system, you will be eligible to start receiving social security benefits at age sixty-two. Assuming you can live off of $30,000 per year, and the markets cooperate, you should have enough to retire on. When you hit sixty-two and start to receive Social Security, you can increase your standard of living, reduce your distribution from savings, or do a little of both.

Now, let's say that instead of retiring at age fifty-five, and living entirely off of your savings, you continue to work until you are sixty-two. You have now retired as soon as you are eligible to receive Social Security. By putting off your retirement for these extra seven years, you will have impacted several areas of your financial security. If the markets cooperated, and you continued to add money to your savings, it could have grown to over $1,000,000 instead of only $500,000. Since you continued to contribute to Social Security, your benefit payments should be higher once you start to take it. Because you have worked longer, you will most likely have fewer years to take distributions from your savings, thus decreasing the chance that you will outlive your money.

So, why have you scrimped and sacrificed to put money into your retirement savings? Was it just so you can die with a big account balance? Of course not; you put that money in there so you could enjoy your retirement. There is no right or wrong time to retire; some times just make better financial sense than others.

How many times have we seen people retire to spend more time with family, or a sick spouse or child? Sometimes, personal circumstances will outweigh the financial advantage of continuing to earn money. Have you ever known someone who retired after they have had a health scare, or were facing a serious illness? When we have a brush with death, we tend to want to slow down and smell the roses.

I have a friend who was a workaholic. He could easily have retired ten years ago, but instead chose to keep working. When he had a brush with cancer he slowed down, started taking time off, and actually enjoying life. He now says that he has never been happier.

How about the people who retire from a job to pursue an alternate career, like golf, fishing, or writing? I actually know of a person who retired from one career and now spends a couple days a week taking people out fishing. He gets paid to do what he loves. Or, there is always the old standard; you have worked long and hard enough; it is time to kick back and enjoy life.

No matter what reason you have for retiring, there are some basic steps that you will want to go through in order to ensure that you have a long and fulfilling retirement that doesn't include your having to ask, "Do you want fries with that?" We will discuss these in more detail in later chapters.

When you retire, there will be several changes. If there weren't, why in the world would you retire?

The biggest change for most people when they retire is the freedom they experience. They no longer have to get up and go to work every day, and must learn what to do with their time. For others, the biggest change will be having to live on less. In some cases, it is much less.

What you want to do in retirement will determine what type of income you will need. Believe it or not, once you retire you might need more income than when you were working. Why, you ask? We have always been told that once you retire you won't need as much income. For many people, their work schedule gets in the way of their leisure pursuits. With work out of the way they are now able to travel, golf, collect art, etc. You want to prepare yourself for the type of retirement you would like to have.

Another substantial change is the loss of health coverage that might occur if you retire before age sixty-five. Health insurance is not a cheap item, especially in the years leading up to age sixty-five. You will need to budget and be prepared to find a health insurance plan to cover you until Medicare kicks in at age sixty-five. That is, if you will be eligible for Medicare.

When you decide it is time to hang it up, and if you are married, you will want to discuss your decision with your spouse. I know this sounds obvious, but you might be surprised at how many times one spouse has come home to break the good news of their retirement to a mortified spouse, who would have liked more time to prepare for this big announcement.

A new trend that I have seen recently is the men retiring, while their wives, who had stayed home to raise the family, join the work force. The reasons are varied and some are kind of funny. I had one wife tell me she didn't think she was ready to spend all of her waking hours with her husband of thirty-six years just yet. She liked to shop at this one particular department store, so she got a job and went to work there. This had many benefits to the couple; she picked up health insurance, made a little extra money, and received a nice discount on clothing she said she would have bought anyway.

Not only does a career later in life add a little bit of money to the budget, it also adds the sense of independence and accomplishment. It establishes an income history, not to mention the creation of new friends that people can make at work.

Just because more people are doing this doesn't mean you have to. I just thought it was an interesting trend.

One of the greatest pitfalls of retirement can be boredom. Once you no longer have to be somewhere, doing something full-time, you can get bored if you don't have hobbies or other activities to occupy your time. Most of my clients tell me that they don't know how they had time to work, because they are so busy in retirement. These people do not have the issues with boredom that many people have when they retire. Their retirement seems to be happier than those people who do suffer from boredom once they retire.

There are several risks linked to boredom; some are physical and mental while others are financial. I have known of at least six people who have lost their life savings in the casinos because they were bored and would head off to the casinos three or four times a week for some "entertainment." Don't think that this can't happen to you because you have too much money saved for your retirement; a couple of them had over $5,000,000 when they retired.

Others turn to the TV, the Internet, or the local bar. If you sit down and don't have to think about anything, your body and brain are not getting any exercise. We all know what happens to something that doesn't get utilized; it starts to deteriorate. If you do not have grandkids close by, a hobby that you look forward to spending more time on, or an organization that you want to be more involved with, you might have a struggle with boredom.

Whether it is volunteering for a cause you are passionate about, or an activity that you love to do, you need something to look forward to that makes you happy. This will give you a more fulfilling life, and possibly even a longer, healthier retirement.

One major factor to consider before you retire is the statistical fact that people are living longer. With joint replacement, medication, and surgical advancement, not only are people living longer, but they are more active and healthier in their retirement years. One surprising statistic I saw on the Social Security website stated that in the last twenty years, retirees have added five years to their life expectancies. I knew that our lives have been extended through medical advances, but that much of an increase was shocking to me. That means, if this trend continues and you retire at sixty-five, your life expectancy will be over ninety years. In the 1940s, when someone retired at age sixty-five, government statistics showed that they were expected to live another four years. What this means to you, is that you no longer need to have your money last four years; you will need to have it last twenty, thirty, or even over forty years.

With people living longer, there are now more activities geared toward seniors than ever before. Just because you get older doesn't mean you won't be able to stay active throughout your life. I had a ninety-year-old client who went canoeing on a fairly swift river. She and her canoe-mate capsized, and she was left in the middle of the river for about ten minutes, clinging onto a log. She was picked up by another passing canoe, and all worked out well. We were all amazed that a ninety-year-old lady would do such a thing. But, we are seeing this type of active behavior more and more every year. People in their eighties, nineties, and even one hundreds are hiking mountains, walking great distances, and leading very active lives. I should mention that the lady in the canoe was very active until her passing at age 104. She was still very sharp mentally as well.

If you do want to hike to the top of a mountain or run a marathon, you might not want to wait until you are ninety. But, you might be able to. Even though you can remain active and accomplish great things, the older you get the more aches and pains you will most likely have to put up with. But, that shouldn't stop you.

Once you retire, you may have some people that you know who will be afraid that you have nothing to do. Many of these people have the best intentions, and they don't want to see you sitting around the house getting stale and bored. If all you do is sit around the house watching TV, these people will invite you to things they are interested in, and volunteer you for causes that they are passionate about. Don't let someone you're not married to orchestrate your life. You haven't worked all these years to be bored. You have plans, things to do, places to go, and people to see.

The fact is, that if you do not do any planning for your retirement, someone else will. Believe it or not, scientific studies have shown that if you do not have control over a situation, you actually have more stress than if you are the person making the decisions. If you let someone else take control of your life in retirement, it will add stress to your life, not to mention that you might not be doing what you really want to do. This added stress will shorten your life expectancy and increase the chances of a long-term illness.

The best way to have control over your circumstances in retirement is to plan. Planning puts the power in your hands so you are not 100 percent dependent on other people. If you have planned for your retirement properly, you should have a sense of independence. This sense of independence helps reduce your stress levels, which will make you less irritable. In turn, that will reduce stress for your spouse, children, and your entire family.

To be really secure and independent you will need to plan a retirement that fits what you want to accomplish, how you want to live and not be in conflict with the values that you aspire to. In other words, you have to plan a retirement based on what you want, not on what some expert that has never met you thinks you should do.

CHAPTER 2

Avoiding the Big Mistakes Close to Retirement

"Mistakes are a fact of life. It is the response to error that counts."
—Nikki Giovanni

One night, as I was watching TV, I came across an episode pertaining to retirement assets on the PBS program *Frontline*. It dealt with the burgeoning 401(k) market, pension plans, and other issues facing pre-retirees. Several things on this program surprised me, but what shocked me most was a story they ran on a couple that had retired. The man had his entire 401(k) assets invested in the stock market, and was planning on retiring soon. When the market dropped in 2000, 2001, and 2002, his account value dropped as well. His 401(k) went from being worth over $200,000 all the way down to about $120,000. He then retired and pulled all of his money out of the 401(k) and paid taxes to the tune of $40,000, since he pulled it all out in one year. Now he was retired, and instead of having over $250,000 in savings to work for him in retirement, he only had around $80,000.

I thought to myself, "Why would anyone do such a thing?" Because I work with many different financial situations, and have worked with and studied the stock market for several years, this was an obvious mistake on several different levels. Surely, it would also be obvious to almost everyone who was invested in stocks. So, I decided to ask some people a question regarding this matter. I gave them the following scenario.

"You are getting ready to retire and your account value is cut in half by a sharp, market drop, what would you do?"

Almost everyone I asked responded in the same way. "Yes, I would sell, because I wouldn't want to lose anymore."

Rule number one when investing for your retirement: "If you are going to take a big loss on your retirement savings, do it when you are young so you have time to recover from your losses."

Rule number two is, "Don't forget rule number one."

A research company called Dalbar did a study on the average return for the average person who invests in the stock market, and compared their returns to the average return of the S&P 500 stock index. The Dalbar 2003 *Quantitative Analysis of Investor Behavior* (QAIB) showed that even though the S & P 500 had a return of 12.22 percent per year from January, 1984 to December, 2002, the average equity investor's return for the same period of time was only 2.57 percent.

This guy's reaction to the falling market is human nature. It happens every time the market goes up or down a significant amount. When the market is setting record highs, I have people calling to buy, and every time the market is taking heavy losses, I have people calling to sell. This is called buying high and selling low.

If you want to make money in the stock market, you have to sell your investments at a price higher than what you paid for them. Otherwise, you guarantee yourself a loss. Losses are bad and should be avoided whenever possible. The question now becomes: "If there are no guarantees in the stock market, how do I avoid taking a loss?"

The answer is simple; you can't. If you want the higher potential return that investing in stocks offers, then you have to accept the risk that at some point in time your investments may be worth less than what you had originally started with. If you are unable or unwilling to accept this risk, you should not invest your money where you have the potential to lose all or part of it. If you are willing to accept the fluctuations in price, then you should allocate your investments. You should do this in such a way that, when the market drops, you don't have to sell something at a loss to provide you with the cash flow that you need.

When you invest in the stock market, you need to expect your account value to go up and down. You need to be prepared for your market investments to take losses that are proportionate to any gains. The stock market most likely won't go to zero; if it does, we have bigger concerns than our retirement savings. If you invest in mutual funds or index funds, you are investing in many different companies. For the market to go to zero, every one of the companies that makes up that index would have to go bankrupt. If you invest all of your money in an individual stock, your account could go to zero because any one company can go bankrupt. In many cases, when a company goes bankrupt, the common shareholder's position gets zeroed out. In other words, the stock you hold in that company becomes worthless. If your entire investment portfolio is made up of stock in one company, the chances of that one stock's value going to zero are much greater than if you have stocks in ten different companies in your portfolio.

If you are afraid that the stock market might drop to zero, and all of your investments in the stock market will become worthless consider this. If all of the companies you had invested your money in were to go out of business, who would you buy your gasoline from? How would you be able to buy clothes, food, and utilities? The same corporations provide most of these items you would invest in if you bought a stock mutual fund or an equity index fund.

So, don't worry about the stock market dropping to zero. Worry about the stock market dropping 50 percent and you having to sell some of your stocks at a big loss because you need the income to live off of.

Now that we know what the problem is, what is the solution? Simple . . . don't invest a large percentage of your assets in the stock market if you aren't prepared to see a long, downward trend in your account value. Make sure you have a source of income somewhere in your portfolio that you can draw money from when you retire, no matter what the stock market does.

Let's think about your retirement assets as a lawnmower. Your lawnmower is only needed when your grass grows tall enough to cut. Your retirement assets are only needed to replace the income you are no longer earning because you have retired.

If you take your lawnmower in to get repaired in December, and the repairman tells you it will be ready in February, are you concerned if it is not repaired by February? Are you concerned even if you will not need it until April? Since it was not ready in February, do you pull it out of that repair shop and move it to another? If you expected it to be finished in February, and it is not, is it acceptable to get concerned and maybe even disappointed?

Sure, it is okay to be concerned and disappointed, I would be. You have expectations, and any time expectations are not met, you tend to get concerned and maybe even frustrated.

What would you do if this were to happen to you? You would probably check with the repair shop to see why it did not get finished when you were expecting it. Remember that you will not need it for at least two more months, so you have plenty of time for the repairs to be made before it is needed. If you move it to another shop, now you have only two months before you need it, and you will go to the back of the line.

Maybe this repairman was moving too slow, and he wouldn't get to it by the time you needed it. But, before you pulled it out of one place and put it into another, wouldn't you check into the reasons why it wasn't done when you expected it?

This is the problem many investors have. When the market drops, their portfolio is not meeting their expectations. Many times these investors will simply pull their investments out of the market and put them somewhere else.

There are times when moving your investments makes perfect sense. For example, if the market has moved up over the last year, and your portfolio did not, you have reason to be concerned. You should do a serious evaluation of your investments if your portfolio doesn't move up when the market moves up, but it goes down when the market goes down.

I have seen mutual funds and portfolios perform like this before. It is usually caused by style drift. Style drift occurs when you do not have a disciplined investment approach. The most obvious case I have seen was in 2000. A successful and well-respected fund manager, who specialized in large cap, value investing, had run a mutual fund for fifteen years. He retired, and a young portfolio manager took his place. She was determined to make up for lost time since the large cap, value stocks were out of favor; the fund she was taking over had not performed as well as large cap, growth stocks did. Can you guess what happened? About the time she got the portfolio converted to large cap, growth stocks, the market shifted. Now, large cap, growth stocks were out of favor and large cap, value stocks were the place to invest. The people who had invested in this fund had not moved up with the market in 1998 and 1999, but they moved down with it in 2000. If she had stayed in large cap, value, the fund would have been up. Instead, her fund was down more than 10 percent. Monitoring a fund when it consistently underperforms is a wise thing to do. It could be because of poor management, or it could be because it is sticking to its discipline. If it is poor management, move the money. If it is because a manager refuses to chase performance, leave the money where it is. Investment cycles come and go, and you never know which as-set category will be the best performer next year.

If you are not going to need the money for eight to ten years, do you need to take drastic action because your portfolio is worth less today than it was yesterday? Are you going to be like that portfolio manager who chased performance and moved the portfolio at the wrong time?

Just like the lawnmower analogy, you want to plan ahead. You wouldn't take your lawnmower in to get it fixed, when you will need it the next day, unless you have another lawnmower to use. When you retire, "the other lawnmower" is simply a source of income. It is a place from which you can take proceeds from that are not tied to the market, just in case there is a large drop.

How do you create this back-up? One way would be to keep enough money in bonds or fixed accounts to provide you with an adequate income for several years, in case the market has a large decline and takes several years to recover.

One of the biggest mistakes people make in the stock market is to take the risk of the downside without the upside potential. That is what happens when you invest money in the stock market and are unable to handle the volatility. You move your money into some-thing "safe," or need the money before the market has time to recover. Having enough safe money to take care of your near-term income needs means you will not have to worry nearly as much about the short-term fluctuations of the stock market.

Here is an example: You invest $100,000 in the stock market. The market takes a large drop and your account is now worth $50,000. You cannot take it any more, and you sell everything and put it into a money market paying 4 percent. In eighteen years, you have now gotten your money back up to $100,000. Meanwhile, if you had left your money in the stock market, it most likely would have been worth much more.

You can use the same example to see how this could negatively impact your retirement income if you depended on that portfolio for income. Let's use the example above. You just retired and are pulling out $10,000 per year to live on. The market drops, and your account loses 50 percent of its value. Now, when you take out the $10,000 you have to sell 20 percent of the portfolio in order to generate the $10,000. How long will your portfolio last under these circumstances?

My wife worked with a lady who wanted to retire early. This lady had read the newsletters and magazines that told her, "Don't pay an advisor; buy no-load funds and do it all yourself." She wanted to learn about "72t," an IRS code that allows you to withdraw money from your retirement account without having to pay the 10 percent penalty for distributions taken before age fifty-nine and a half. She asked me some questions regarding this topic, and inquired about what funds she should invest in. I told her the resources she should utilize, but informed her that I couldn't provide her with the information she wanted because of industry regulation and liability purposes.

Unfortunately, she didn't have the interest or the understanding to become a do-it-yourselfer. She overestimated her return, and because of that, she wasn't able to sustain her requirement for her 72t distribution for the five years that she was required to do so under the law. She wound up not only losing all of her money, but also being in debt to the IRS for the 10 percent penalty on the money she had withdrawn prior to age fifty-nine and a half.

She could have avoided this situation in a couple of ways. She could have not put all of her money in the stock market, thinking she could get an easy 15 percent per year. Or, she could have gotten professional advice to help her figure out a sensible amount of money to withdraw from her retirement savings.

Figuring out how much money you can take out of your IRA to

satisfy a 72t distribution, without depleting it, is more difficult than simply planning for a drop in the stock market. A drop in the stock market is a natural event that will occur from time to time. If you are taking money out of your IRA after you turn fifty-nine, you can simply reduce the amount you are receiving to match the drop in your account value. You know a drop in the market is going to happen eventually; you just need to be prepared for it when it happens.

When taking an early retirement, you will need to plan an investment allocation that will allow you to receive the income you need without depleting your account. You will also need to know the proper laws to follow for your distribution strategy. One mistake could cost you your retirement income.

If you are going to do it yourself, you will have to learn the rules and regulations so you don't wind up owing the IRS money unnecessarily. If you are in a situation where you plan to retire before fifty-nine, and you plan on doing it yourself, find a good advisor to review your plan to make sure that you are on the right track. It might cost you a few thousand dollars, but if it prevents you from losing your retirement savings, it might be the best money you ever spent.

The last common mistake that I will cover is one that has cost thousands of pre-retirees their entire retirement savings, yet it continues to happen almost every year.

This can happen when an employee has put all or most of their retirement account's value into the company's stock. We all remember the stories about Enron and WorldCom and how their employees had put so much money into the company stock within their 401(k) plans, only to lose it all.

If you are a pre-retiree who plans on retiring in two or three years, just think about the impact your company going out of business will have on your retirement.

Let's say you are sixty years old and you want to retire when you are sixty-two. You have $500,000 in your 401(k), and most of that is invested in your company's stock. If the company goes bankrupt, you lose your investment in the company's stock and you also have just lost your job.

So, now do you retire early with almost no savings, or do you try to find another job and work for the next fifteen years to build up your 401(k) again?

To take it one step further, what happens if you had a pension through the now bankrupt company. Although you will still receive a pension payment, it might be at a reduced rate.

Even if your company doesn't go bankrupt, you still are at risk of making a significant negative impact on your retirement security. If you worked for IBM in the 1990s, then you know they had a reputation of never laying off employees. This all changed when they hit hard times. Their stock went from over $100 per share to less than $40, and they started laying people off. Many managers were in their fifties and sixties. So, now you have just gone from having a big, retirement nest egg, and a secure job, to being unemployed. Your nest egg is worth less than half of what it was just a few months before.

Is this what you had planned for?

After talking to pre-retirees who have a big position of company stock in their 401(k), it seems they usually have the same answer. "The company I work for is not going belly up. Besides, I know this company better than any other."

Are you certain of that? Are you going to get a better return from your company's stock than you could from another allocation strategy?

Do you know what the following companies all have in common?
Penn Central Railroad
International Harvester
Western Union
The Great Atlantic and Pacific Tea Company (A&P)
Pan AM

Polaroid

Woolworth

Colt Firearms

Kmart

Arthur Anderson

According to Wikipedia.com, all of these companies were either the largest or second largest companies in their industry at one point in time, and they have all gone bankrupt. Some were long and drawn-out declines, and some were rather quick and unexpected.

It's a fact that you can never be certain of what will happen to the company you are working for between now and the time you retire. Why take the risk of having all of your eggs in one basket?

Company stock does have tremendous upside potential, but you need to manage the risk prudently, especially the closer you get to retirement.

Yes, it is true that most people who have become millionaires while working for a company have done it through the company stock plan. Microsoft, Wal-Mart, and Google are some great examples of this. But, with great opportunity also comes great risk.

The people who have become millionaires with companies like these typically started working at the companies when these firms were relatively small and growing rapidly. Once the companies had matured, and their growth rates had slowed, their stocks usually have not performed as well as they once had.

For example: If you worked for Walmart when they first offered stock to the public in 1970, and had invested $10,000 in the company stock plan, your investment would have grown to around $1.4 million over the next twenty years.

Had you invested $10,000 in the same plan in 1988, and held it until 2008 your money would have grown to about $160,000. This is still a good rate of return, but not nearly as good as it was when the company was much younger.

You could make the same example of Microsoft, Intel, or most other successful companies out there, for that matter.

I have a client who went to work for a small company as a salesperson. She received stock options as part of her benefits package when she first started working there. After a few years of working at this company, the price of the stock moved up dramatically. We discussed the different possibilities for her stock options. The safest thing to do would be to sell the options as soon as we were able, but the most potential for wealth would be to hold the options and the stock as long as possible.

I suggested a compromise; we would sell some shares and keep a majority of the shares for long-term appreciation. She was fairly young and could work many more years if she needed to. If the stock worked out well, she could retire early using this strategy. The stock did well, and she retired after a few years with a very nice nest egg. Now she is set for a very secure retirement. If she had held onto all of the stocks as long as possible she would have wound up with a couple million dollars more. But, she wound up with several hundred thousand more than she would have if we had sold the stocks as soon as possible.

I had another client who had a very similar situation. She had a large number of shares of another small but growing company. She would sell a few shares if she needed a new roof or a car, but never sold any significant amount of this stock.

The stock continued to increase in value and was eventually worth over $1,300,000. We tried to get her to sell most or all of the stock, due to the fact that she hated her job and wanted to retire as soon as possible. She had seen her investment go from being worth $24,000 to $1,300,000 in about seven short years. She was thinking the stock would be worth $5,000,000 one day, and didn't want to leave any money on the table by selling too early.

Can you guess what happened? The stock started to drop in value and it continued to drop. When it went from $60 per share down to

$50, she said she would sell when it went back up to $60. When it hit $40 a share, her stocks value was under a million dollars, so she said she would sell it when the stock got back up over a million. When it was $1.87, she wished she had sold it earlier.

You can find hundreds of examples just like these where people have made or lost millions through company stock plans. A question to ask yourself, if you have a lot of money in your company's stock, is this: "What will happen to my retirement plan if this stock doesn't do well? Will it dramatically improve my life if this stock does well?"

Greed tends to cloud your judgment, leading you to try and get that one big score before you retire. I feel this is one of the biggest risks for people getting close to retirement . . . putting their entire retirement savings at risk to try to make a little (or most times, a lot) more money. We actually have seen this happen quite often. Someone has a comfortable amount of money set aside and they want more, so they take big risks with the hope for a big return. They forget to consider the downside potential of this extra risk, and expose themselves to the possibility of a large drop in account values.

The more upside potential you have usually means the more downside risk you have to take.

Can you strike it rich with company stock or an aggressive stock portfolio? You sure can. You can also strike it rich with the lottery, but you don't want to pin your retirement hopes on it.

To summarize; if you have most or all of your savings in your 401(k), and you plan on retiring soon, make sure you have at least four year's worth of income put into some fixed income investments. This way, if there is a long market correction, you will not have to sell a large portion of your portfolio at a loss to fund current income needs. Don't keep a large percentage of your total assets in your company's stock.

Don't risk your future financial security on the hopes for a big score in the market.

CHAPTER 3
Preparing For Retirement

"Forewarned, forearmed; to be prepared is half the victory."
—Miguel de Cervantes Saavedra

I have a client who came in to see me. He is in excellent health, and was really hoping he could afford to retire.

He said to me, "I just don't know if I can take it any longer. I hate getting up and going into the office every day. I have been doing this for thirty-five years, and I have done well. I have moved up the ladder like I was supposed to. I just don't want to go any higher and don't want to continue what I am doing anymore."

I told him that if he was not able to retire at this time, he should at least consider a different career.

If you hate your job, and don't like going into work, you need to change something. If you can't afford to retire, the least you should do is change careers.

Some people are in no hurry to retire because they are happy working. These people are afraid that if they don't retire they will, "die with their boots on."

One of the biggest considerations to retirement is "What kind of lifestyle can I afford to have if I retire now?" And a better question might be, "Can I afford the lifestyle I would like to have if I retire now?"

In 1997, while on our honeymoon, my wife Patti and I went to St. Lucia in the British West Indies. I met a man there who was obviously not a native. He appeared to be in his mid-forties and had adopted the "no hurry, no worry, no problem" attitude of the island. He was an American who, in his thirties, got tired of the rat race. He had visited the island and fell in love with it. This person sold everything he had, and paid cash for a house on the island. In 1997, you could buy a nice little bungalow on a hill overlooking the Caribbean for about $30,000. According to our driver, you could buy other houses for under $10,000 that were livable. After the house purchase, he had around $27,000 left in savings. I asked him how he could afford to live on so little savings. He said that it was very cheap to live there, and as long as he didn't have a car or repairs to his house, he could live on the interest from his savings.

This is a lifestyle choice; he gave up all luxuries, including electricity, and went to live on a tropical island. In order to save money he gathered much of his own food from the island. He ate a lot of fish and bananas. Most of us reading this would never dream of giving up our lives of luxury for such a simple life, while others will think it is an ideal way to retire.

Once again, we see that one person's paradise is another person's purgatory. There is no retirement that is ideal for everyone. So, when you hear a retirement expert say those same old statements about how you need to be able to generate 60 to 70 percent of your current income once you retire; think about how you want to retire.

Although the "retire early to a tropical island and live in paradise" option sounds good, there is a potential problem to consider before choosing this retirement plan. It is called, "What happens when the unexpected happens?" For example, what would he do if his cost of living went up dramatically, or if the interest he received from his savings went down dramatically? Would his small amount of savings still be covering his expenses? What happens if he is afflicted with an illness and can no longer gather his own food? How would he buy his food and medicine if he lives to be one hundred and ten? Don't laugh; more people are hitting that mark every year.

I know this is an extreme example. I thought it was an interesting choice, and wanted to show you each end of the spectrum. I have seen people try to retire in a manner similar to this from time to time. They will retire early, try to maximize their resources, and hope and pray nothing unexpected happens.

I had a lady in my office whose husband had retired early. He thought he could withdraw 10 percent from his 401(k) each year, and still have good enough performance that his account would continue to grow. In order for them to live the lifestyle they wanted, and still retire early, they needed to take the 100 percent pension with no spousal benefit. What this means is that, as soon as he dies, his pension is gone and his spouse gets nothing. The reason they did it this way was that if they chose the spousal benefit, they would only get $1,200 per month. Without the spousal benefit, they were able to receive $1,600 per month. He had roughly $200,000 in his 401(k). So, he was taking $20,000 per year out of the 401(k) per year, and they had $19,200 coming in from pension. They were living on almost half of what he was making before, but in nine years they could both draw Social Security. Three years into retirement the market dropped, and it continued to drop. The husband died and the pension went away; the account was now worth less than $130,000. His wife wanted to know how we could replace the pension and still receive the $20,000 from the retirement savings.

The only financial advice I could give her was to find a job, go to work, replace that income, and minimize her expenses.

This is a sad case, but far from isolated. If you have a spouse that will rely on your pension if you die first, consider your options carefully. We never know how long we will live, so plan as if you could die tomorrow, or forty years from now, because they are both true.

You do not know what type of income you will need until you decide what type of lifestyle you want to have when you retire. In the two cases I just told you about, there was a common mistake. They didn't have a backup plan if things didn't work out the way they had hoped. The guy on St. Lucia was young enough that if financial catastrophe were to strike, he could easily go back to work as long as it happened while he was still healthy enough. When you are older, going back to work becomes more difficult and your employment options become fewer.

So, you come home from work and say those five magic words, "Honey I want to retire." The first thought that usually runs through one's head at this time is, "Wow, sounds great, can we afford to retire?" If you're not thinking about whether you can afford to retire or not, you should be.

A good trial run is simple; decide what you want to do in retirement. Sitting around watching TV and watching each other grow old is not a good option. How many trips do you want to take each year? What costs will you still have once you retire? Where will you live? Consider all of your possibilities, give a good estimate on what they will cost, and don't be conservative. Remember the new kitchen that turned out to cost twice as much as you anticipated? Don't forget inflation. Once you have figured out how much you think you will need to live on, try it out for a year. Make a budget and see if your expectations are realistic or not. By trying it for a year you will get the full cycle of expenses that we often overlook when budgeting, such as taxes, dues, and insurance.

Make a budget. If you are going to travel, figure out how much your trips will cost. Factor in the cost of a second home, as well as all of these items you have on your wish list to do when you retire. Put an anticipated cost on them, and make your budget as realistic as you can.

Once you have a realistic assessment of what you will need to live on, figure out how much you will have in income.

This method is known as a "Bottoms Up" approach. This technique works best when you have flexible plans for retirement.

Let's say you have figured out everything you want to do in retirement, and it will cost $100,000 per year. You look at your current savings, pension, and Social Security, and they total $60,000. You could simply continue to work until you are able to bring your retirement income up to the $100,000 number that you want. Don't forget inflation, which has historically been around 4 percent on average. So, for every year that goes by you will probably need to increase your income need by around 4 percent.

Remember, it is never too late to start saving for your retirement. I was giving a presentation to a group of workers when one of the people in the audience made the statement, "I haven't got much set aside and I am retiring in seven years, so there is no need to start now."

I asked what her current household income was, and she told me it was about $68,000 per year. I asked how much their income would be in retirement, and she said it would be a little over $30,000 with pension and social security. I asked her how she and her husband would do on $38,000 less per year in income.

Her response was, "We will make it; we have no choice. I'm not working until I am seventy."

She was fifty-eight and planned to work until sixty-five, and her husband planned to do the same. I suggested that they try to live on $30,000 per year just to see what it would be like to live on so little. I also suggested that if they could just cut their expenses to $40,000 per year, and put the additional $28,000 per year difference into savings, they would have over $200,000 in additional savings when they retired. With the additional savings, they could generate enough extra income to have a $40,000 per year income.

By taking this approach, two things would be accomplished. First, it would dramatically increase their savings. Second, it would let them experience what it would be like to live on the income they will have once they retire. Trying out your retirement income is an important thing to do. It allows you to experience the lifestyle you can afford, and decide before you retire whether or not this lifestyle is acceptable. If it is not acceptable, and you have already retired, will you be able to find a job paying as much as you did before you retired? It can be challenging, in many cases, for a retiree to come out of retirement and earn as much or more money than they did before they retired. This is because many things change over the course of several years. Your skills might not match what is currently needed in the work place, or you might not want to take on the demands of a full-time job that you had when you were younger.

Another significant item in this example, one that most people overlook, is that this pension is fixed. When this woman retires, her $30,000 annual income will buy less and less each year because of inflation.

This approach is known as the "Top Down" approach. You see how much money you will have and decide what things you can afford to do when you retire. On $30,000 per year you might get to do everything you wanted to do in retirement, or it might just be enough to provide food and shelter. It depends on your lifestyle. The top down approach works best if you have less flexibility in your retirement.

When she implements this plan, she might realize that she and her husband don't want to make that many sacrifices. They might continue working for a few more years to accumulate more, or they might decide that they can live on $30,000 per year and not need to do any additional planning.

Your income in retirement will most likely come from four places: Social Security, savings, investments, and possibly a pension.

If you have a pension through your employer, the human resources department should be able to help you figure out the amount of income that the pension should provide to you once you retire. Likewise, the Social Security office can help you figure your Social Security income, and when you will be eligible to receive it. Don't forget that, if you have a spouse that has made substantially less than you, they will receive approximately one half as much Social Security as you do.

Figuring out much income you will receive from your retirement savings is a little more complicated. Due to fluctuating markets, and the different tax levels for different types of savings, it will be more challenging for you to set a realistic income measure for your time frame and comfort level. Many experts feel that 4 percent is a realistic figure to receive from your retirement savings if you retire at sixty-five. If you retire when you are over sixty-five you can withdraw a higher percentage of your savings than if you retire when you are under sixty-five. Methods and examples of how to calculate a reasonable income from your savings will be covered in greater detail in the reference section at the end of this book.

The reason it is better for you to withdraw a lower percentage of your retirement savings, when you retire at a younger age, is simple. The earlier you retire, the longer your money is going to have to last. If you start pulling out more money than your account earns, your principal will decrease. The smaller your account value, the less it is capable of earning. It works just like compound interest, only in reverse. The less principal you have, the higher the percentage of assets you need to take in order to keep your income the same. Hopefully, if you do find yourself in this situation, you can reduce your assets at a slow enough pace that you don't run out of money in your lifetime.

Usually, people will pull out more income than their accounts earn due to poor market performance or decreasing interest rates. When these occur you have three choices:

1. Reduce the income you are taking from the account.
2. Try to increase your return, usually resulting in taking more risk.
3. Do nothing.

Option three works fine if you have a short time horizon; option one is the choice that tends to be the most effective.

Let's say you have $1,000,000 in retirement savings and you are going to take out $70,000 per year from the total portfolio. If your investments average a 5 percent return, without any negative returns, for the first ten years, you will have to dip into principal to maintain the $70,000 per year. At the end of this ten-year period, your savings is down to under $800,000. If you had retired when you were seventy, there is a very good chance that you could continue taking your $70,000 distribution per year without running out of money in your lifetime. In this situation, you have enough money to maintain your income for the next eleven years, even if there is no growth in your portfolio. So, for you to run out of money you would need a combination of a really long life and large market losses.

Had you retired when you were fifty, and had the same thing happened, your portfolio would be down to $800,000 by the time you were sixty. Your portfolio would need to average an almost 9 percent return per year in order to maintain your income without continuing to deplete your assets.

Is there a chance your portfolio could average over 9 percent per year? Sure there is, but you would probably need to have most of the portfolio in more aggressive investments to accomplish that type of return.

After reading the example I just gave, many of you might be thinking that for a 5 percent return, you are not going to take the risk of the stock market. You will just put all of your money in conservative investments such as bonds or certificates of deposit. If your plan is to only invest in very conservative investments, you should withdraw an even lower percentage of your assets than you would if you had some of your funds invested in stocks. Even though you are not concerned about loss of principal due to market fluctuations with bonds and certificates of deposit, you do need to be concerned about loss of purchasing power and interest rate risk.

Interest rate risk is simply the risk that, when fixed income investments are redeemed, you will not able to replace those investments at the same interest rate. Therefore, you will suffer a decrease in earnings. A quick example is as follows.

You buy a bond that yields 7 percent, investing $100,000 into this bond. Therefore, each year you receive $7000. The bond matures, and the best rate you can find for an equivalent bond is 5 percent. You have just experienced a drop in income of $2000 per year. This is the case whether a bond is called away or matures.

Bonds will often have a call feature; this allows the issuer to "call" the bond before it matures. In other words, they can redeem the bond on any call date before it matures.

Using the same example as above, what happens if you retire with $1,000,000 in savings? Let's say you invest it all in a number of bonds and C/Ds, and you are able to average 7 percent per year on your interest. If you decide to withdraw all of your interest, you will take, on average, $70,000 per year. If interest rates drop and you have a number of bonds mature or get called away from you early, what are you going to do? Will you reduce your income, or will you start using the principal to fund your distributions? If you retired when you were fifty-five, what impact would inflation have on your distributions?

Take this scenario, for example. If you had retired in 1981 with $100,000, and invested that full amount in a thirty year Treasury bond yielding 14 percent, you would have been making $14,000 per year just off of the interest from your bond. In 1981, most people could have lived comfortably off of $14,000 per year income. How well could you live off of $14,000 per year now? What interest will you receive when this bond matures and you have to re-invest the proceeds? If you were to invest the proceeds from your bond maturing now, you would most likely get less than $7,000 per year income. If you can't imagine trying to live on $14,000 per year now, how about trying to live on $7,000?

A more common occurrence is that people don't prepare for drops in interest rates. One time, when I worked with a number of insurance agents, I sat next to an older gentleman who had never invested in the stock market because it was too risky. He only invested in short term C/Ds and Treasury notes. He was older, so he didn't want any longer maturities; everything he bought had to mature in less than five years. He didn't plan for a drop in interest rates, and in 1992, when short-term interest rates dropped to under 3 percent he was stressed. All of a sudden his income supplement had dropped by 70 percent. I heard him calling banks all day long, trying to get a higher interest rate. Rates finally started to move higher in 1994, but for two years he had to withdraw some of his principal to live on while he waited for interest rates to move higher.

He could have lessened the negative effects of lower interest rates by simply locking in an interest rate for a longer period of time. This is done by simply investing in longer maturing bonds.

Many people don't want to own bonds that mature in ten to thirty years because they are afraid of dying before these bonds mature. I hate to tell you this, but unless you only invest in money market accounts, or all of your bonds mature the day before you die, you are going to die owning some bonds. This is not a big deal; your heirs and beneficiaries can sell these bonds or they can keep them until they mature or are called.

No matter how you choose to invest your retirement savings there will always be some sort of risk involved, even if you only invest all of your savings in bonds or C/Ds.

One of the most common mistakes made by retirees is pulling too much from their savings each year. According to SunGard Analytics, the Dow Jones Industrial Average has averaged over 10 percent per year from 1987 to 2007. Too often people will assume they can withdraw 8 percent to 10 percent from their savings and investments each year, because the Dow Jones Industrials have averaged over 10 percent per year. If you had listened to some of the people giving advice on radio and TV in the late 90s, you would have heard comments such as, "Any allocation should begin and end with the S&P 500," "If you buy an index fund you have all of the diversification that you need," "You shouldn't withdraw over 7 percent or 8 percent per year in case the market should go down," or "Since people are spending more time in retirement than they used to, you should invest less in bonds and more in stocks."

Let's see what would have happened if you had followed this advice and had retired in 2000. Almost everyone was optimistic about the market because the Internet was going to change everything, so a 15 percent annual return was thought to be realistic by many people. You retire on January 1, 2000, and invest your entire retirement savings into an S&P 500 index fund. This is all the money you have, so you want to play it safe. So, you only withdraw 7 percent per year of your account value.

Do you know how much you would have left in your account now? Your account value would have declined so much that you would either have to go back to work or dramatically reduce your income. As a hypothetical example, if you had put $1,000,000 into the S&P 500 index, and withdrawn $70,000 per year from January 1, 2000, to June 30, 2008, your account would have been worth about $355,000 at the end of that period. If you had pulled out $80,000 per year over the same time frame, your account would be down to about $262,000. This includes reinvesting all dividends.

Before you get discouraged, and decide never to retire because of the risk of running out of money, let's assume instead that you had retired on January 1, 1993. You had the same $1,000,000 and you pulled out $80,000 per year. If you invested everything into an S&P 500 index fund, your account would have grown to about $1,650,000 on June 30, 2008.

This is known as "sequence of return risk." Simply stated, how your investments perform at the beginning of your distribution is more important than how your investments perform at the end.

If you are wondering how this works, it is really quite simple. If you invest your money in an investment, and that investment grows at a faster rate than your distributions, then your account will grow. When your account is going down not only is your account value dropping due to market performance, but also you are taking funds out of your account, causing the value to go down even further.

To illustrate how this works, let's say that on January 1, 1995, you put $100,000 in a fund that would produce $15,000 per year in gains for five years. Now, this is a made-up fund, nothing at this time will guarantee you this type of return; I am just using this for illustrative purposes.

You are retired, so you will need income from your retirement savings. Thus, you withdraw from this fund $7000 per year. Since the fund is earning more than you are taking out, it will grow each year. At the end of 1995, you would have $108,000. At the end of 1996, you would have $116,000. The growth would have continued until the end of 1999, when you would have had $140,000 in your account. You would have been retired five years, and your account would have been up $40,000 more than what you had started with. You would have withdrawn $35,000, and obviously had chosen a good time to retire.

Now, let's use the same figures for a different scenario. Instead of retiring in 1995 when the market was roaring, you retire on January 1, 2000. Many people were more optimistic about the market in 2000 than they were in 1995, so your expectations might have been even higher. No matter how optimistic people were, you still wanted to keep your distributions at the same $7,000 per year. The only thing that changed was that instead of the market going up for the first few years you were retired, it went down. Let's assume that, with the market drop, your fund lost $10,000 per year in value (due to market fluctuations) for three years. Once again, this is an illustration, not an actual investment.

At the end of 2000, your account would have been down to $83,000 ($10,000 market loss plus $7000 income distribution). In addition, you would not only have had the market loss market loss, you would have had the income that you were taking out. By the end of 2001, your account would have been down to $66,000, and at the end of 2002 your account would have dropped to $49,000. There is a slim chance that you would have seen a market turnaround that would have allowed you to continue to receive your $7000 income from this fund for the rest of your life, but you would have felt much less secure than you did when you first retired.

Two ways to help protect you from a situation like the second example would be to withdraw a smaller percentage of your account. You could also have a portion of your portfolio invested in bonds, or some other fixed income product designed to produce income. These are typically not as volatile as stocks.

The volatility of the stock markets makes them an efficient way to invest money on a systematic basis. However, this volatility can make them very inefficient to withdraw funds from.

Would you rather run out of money early in retirement, or later, or not at all?

You should sit down with a qualified investment professional that has the resources and knowledge to help you plan an appropriate allocation strategy. This will allow you to see how much income you can expect to safely receive from your savings. You can do this yourself, but be very conservative and don't plan on taking more than 6 percent income from your portfolio.

A good resource to check the security of your income is a "Monte Carlo Simulation," model or some similar distribution simulation model. These simulation models show you what the likelihood is that your portfolio will remain intact for your lifetime. These models do not guarantee performance, and do not depict an investment in any particular product.

If your employer offers health care and a pension, then personal retirement planning could be much easier for you; and you may be able to get by with much less in savings in order to retire comfortably. Even if you do have health care and a good pension, there are still several things you will want to have before you retire.

There are several factors to look at when you have a pension. The two most important things to consider are whether the monthly payments increase with inflation and the financial strength of the organization providing the pension.

A pension that is indexed to inflation will increase the payments each year, reducing the need for you to supplement your pension, due to inflation, with outside income later in life. Inflation is something most people forget to consider; most pensions that I have seen are not indexed to inflation.

Here is why it is important to plan for the effects of inflation on your income. If you retire at age sixty-five and are married (according to the actuarial estimates by the Social Security Administration as of 2006) there is over a 50 percent chance that either you or your spouse will live to be ninety. If you would have retired in 1982 at age sixty-five, according to the Bureau of Labor Statistics, you would have paid $0.90 for a gallon of gasoline; a stamp was $0.20, and the average monthly rent was $320. In 2008, a stamp costs $0.42 a gallon of gasoline is over $3.50 a gallon, and I don't know what kind of house you could rent for $320 per month. This does not even take into consideration that many of your other expenses could increase at a faster rate when you get older. Some of the items I am talking about are health care, medication, and long-term care.

Just because you have a pension doesn't mean you still shouldn't have some funds set aside for emergencies, and to supplement your income.

When planning on retiring, be conservative with your assumptions; assume your income will be lower and your expenses will be higher. The longer you work, the greater the chance your portfolio will remain intact throughout your life. Don't forget inflation; the younger you retire the greater impact inflation will have on your retirement savings.

CHAPTER 4

Where Will the Money Come From?

"I never stopped doing anything [when I retired], I stopped getting paid for it."

— Bill Chavanne

I read a fascinating report about the percentage of people who will outlive their money. Ernst and Young did the report in 2008. They found that three out of five middle-class-workers would try to maintain too high a standard of living in retirement, causing them to run out of money. The study was very interesting in the fact that certain areas had a higher probability of retirees running out of money than others. They attributed this to fixed pensions. The more people covered by fixed pensions, the less likely they were to outlive their assets. They also discovered that the later people retired, the less likely they would be to run out of money.

What this study showed me is the importance of having reasonable expectations regarding the return on your investments. Many people think they will receive a higher income from their investments than they actually will. This gives people the idea that they can live a higher lifestyle than they should. It also leads to people spend more from their retirement savings than the savings can replace.

Think of your savings as a bucket. When you are working and saving, you are adding water to your bucket. Once you retire you stop putting water into this bucket, and instead you start to take water out of this bucket. As you start to take a steady stream of income from your retirement savings, it is as if you have just poked a hole in the bucket and a steady stream of water is running out. Your hope is that the water going into the bucket (growth, interest, and dividends) is more than the water seeping out, or that there is enough water in the bucket to last you for your lifetime. Anytime you take additional distributions from your retirement account it is the same as reaching in and scooping some water out of the bucket. The more you reach into the bucket to scoop water out, the sooner the bucket runs out of water. If the market does well you get more water put into your bucket, but if the market does poorly you get water taken away.

The more water you have in the bucket, and the smaller the holes you make in the bucket, the better chance that your money will outlive you and not the other way around.

It is important to have as big a bucket as possible before you retire, because you will most likely need to provide for yourself in retirement.

Retirement has changed a lot over the last fifty years. It used to be that you went to work for a company, and after forty years you retired and lived off of the company pension and Social Security for the rest of your life.

According to the Pension Research Council, approximately 20 percent of all private sector employees were covered by a company pension in 2005. That number is down from 40 percent in 1980. With a number of the larger companies in this country freezing or eliminating their pension plans, the percentage of employees covered by traditionally defined, benefit pension plans will continue to drop.

What does this mean to you? If you are not one of the fortunate few people covered by a pension, then you will be responsible for creating your own "pension." Companies have started to replace their defined benefit pension plans with 401(k)s. These are known as defined contribution plans. A traditional pension is a defined benefit plan. You work for a company a certain number of years, and earn a certain amount of money. They will pay you a defined amount when you retire. The company has to guarantee this amount to its retirees. If the pension plan investments underperform, the company has to make up the difference. In a defined contribution plan, the company only needs to guarantee the contributions, not the performance. Because of this, 401(k)s are less expensive to administer than traditional pension plans. The employer has much less risk associated with managing a 401(k) versus a traditional pension plan.

Whether you are going to be covered by a traditional pension or not, some amount of planning is still going to be required to help insure that you have the resources necessary to retire comfortably.

Social Security does have an annual increase called a Cost of Living Adjustment (COLA). This COLA is supposed to offset the effects of inflation on your Social Security income over your lifetime. Many would argue that the COLA calculation for Social Security doesn't accurately depict the increased cost of living of retirees.

Let's assume you retire with a fixed pension whose amount will never go up. If you are going to maintain your standard of living throughout retirement, you will want to have some additional savings so you can offset the effect inflation will have on your purchasing power as the years go by. The younger you are when you retire, the more impact inflation will have on your later years.

When sitting down with people who are planning retirement, one of the major questions is, "Where is the money going to come from?" Whether it is 401(k), pension, inheritance, or lottery, a plan still has to be made to see if the standard of living people envision is in line with the resources they will have.

Don't think just because you won $50,000,000 in the lottery you can't go broke before you die; many people have already proved it can be done.

Let's start by adding up all of your income sources. This could include pensions, 401(k), royalties, social security, annuities, and rent. Factor in absolutely every source from which you will receive income after you retire. Don't forget that your spouse is entitled to approximately half of your Social Security benefits, even if they didn't work.

Once you have all of these sources listed, add up your income. Does it look like you have enough to live on? If so, you are in good shape. If not, you have some work to do.

Two sources that people tend to overlook or overestimate are their house and their inheritance.

If you live in a house that you plan on selling, it should be considered an asset that can help you generate retirement income. That is, it will generate retirement income as long as you are going to buy a house that is dramatically less expensive than the one you currently own. This is not always the case.

I have a couple of clients whose kids had moved out; they lived in a nice, 2,500 square-foot house where they raised their children. They were planning on moving into a smaller house that was cheaper and easier for them to maintain. It turns out that they found a 3,500 square-foot Victorian house that they fell in love with. Needless to say, this house wasn't less expensive or easier to maintain than their previous home.

A house is a wonderful thing to have, and is almost a necessity, but they are seldom a great investment. Before you start thinking that I have lost my mind–because you know that the house you bought for $40,000 some forty years ago is now worth $500,000–

please hear me out. Many people are pushing the idea of buying the most expensive house you can to help you build assets. According to a 2007 "cost of home-ownership" study from Fannie Mae, and the Office of Federal Housing Enterprise Oversight (OFHEO), the average homebuyer is at about break even for the house they bought thirty years ago as their primary residence.

Even though the house you bought twenty-five years ago cost $75,000, and now is worth $300,000, how much did you have to pay in taxes, maintenance, heating, cooling, interest, and improvements?

The bigger the house, the higher the payments, and the more you have to spend on furniture, taxes, upkeep, and utilities. The main reason you build so much equity in a house is because it is a forced savings plan. You have to put money into the house or it will fall in or be repossessed.

Almost every client I have with over a million dollars in investments lived in a modest house during their accumulation period. They spent less on houses and put more into their savings; this strategy paid off nicely for them.

I am not saying that buying a house is a bad investment; what I am saying is that thinking that your house is a good retirement plan might not be the best idea. A house is a place to live and raise a family, make memories, and a place to call home.

We will look into the true cost of housing in the reference section of this book. For now, I just wanted to cover the basics.

Inheritance cannot be counted on for several reasons. You never know when you will get disinherited. Your parents might be around for a long time, and they might spend every dime they ever saved before they die. This tends to happen more often when they move into an assisted living facility. Such care often costs more than what they are earning, and they must dip into savings to pay for it.

We have a client whose father was well off. Sometime in his seventies, the father decided to re-marry. After the marriage to the second wife, the father revised his trust to allow his second wife to receive income from his trust as long as she lived. She would also be able to take out principal from the trust for emergencies. You can probably imagine what happened. She had an "emergency" that required the full balance of the trust. So, the children who were approaching retirement, and thought they each had a couple million coming to them, wound up with nothing.

Don't think that this type of thing doesn't happen in the real world; it does. I have several friends who are attorneys who deal with this type of thing. They say it happens on a fairly regular basis.

Even if you have parents with a lot of money, don't spend it until you have it in your hands. I have seen people go into debt expecting a big inheritance, and then not receive enough to pay off what they owed when their parents passed on. Don't count on inheritance until the estate settles.

While we are on the topic of planning for something that might not be, let's talk about company pensions.

Why is the financial strength of the company or union paying your pension important to consider? You might think, "Yes, but my pension is guaranteed by the government."

You would be correct, the federal government does have a program to protect your pension in case the organization backing it up should go bankrupt; it's called the Pension Benefit Guarantee Corporation.

We were able to see how this system worked in 2001-2003, when so many large companies that had offered pensions to their employees were going bankrupt. In a case where the company goes bankrupt, the Pension Benefit Guarantee Corporation (PBGC) steps in to ensure that the participant's pension payments will continue. However, in many cases the payments are reduced; in some cases they are reduced substantially. The United Airlines case comes to mind. In a report I saw on the PBS program, *Frontline*, regarding retirement, several United Airline retirees were interviewed. One individual's pension had started out at $2,100 per month, and his benefit had not been reduced by that much. The next person they interviewed had a pension of over $4,500 per month; his payments dropped substantially. This tends to be the case with most of the people who have had pensions with companies that go bankrupt. The people who had the smaller pensions (under $3,000 per month) tended to receive a higher percentage of their original pension payment from the PBGC. The people who had the larger pensions (over $3,000 per month) tended to get a smaller percentage of their original payment.

How do you deal with a situation where you work for a company whose financial strength is questionable, and you are relying on their pension to help you retire? If your company offers a pension buy-out at retirement, you might be able to take the buyout and put the proceeds into a similar investment, such as a single-premium, immediate annuity from a highly rated insurance company.

If this is your situation, you should contact your human resources department to see how much your pension buy-out would be. Once you know how much you could receive from your pension buy-out, you get a quote for a joint-life, single-premium, and immediate annuity from a highly rated insurance company.

If the monthly payment is the same or higher than your company's pension payments, then it is a "no brainer." However, if your payments would be reduced by taking the buy-out you would need to reconsider. You might be better off taking your chances with the payment that the PBGC would provide to you if your company was to go bankrupt.

Another thing to consider is that the PBGC does not guarantee any other benefits that your company might provide retirees, such as life or health insurance. These will be additional expenses that you will want to consider when calculating your expenses.

Once you have figured out how much income you expect to receive in retirement, do you think you could live off of this amount? Is it more or less than you currently earn? If your retirement income will be higher than your current income, you are in great shape. If it is less than your current income, try to live on an amount equal to the amount you will live on in retirement. See how comfortable your lifestyle is.

To try this experiment, set up your current income so that it is equal to what your retirement income will be. You can do this fairly easily by taking the extra money that you currently earn and putting it into some sort of savings.

Here is an example. Let's say you currently earn $70,000 per year. Of that amount, you put $10,000 into savings. Your adjusted gross income is now $60,000 ($70,000 of earnings minus $10,000 savings). Note that this example does not take into consideration taxes or the effect of taxes on pre/post retirement income.

Now, let's look at the income you will have in retirement. Let's say you will have $22,000 per year coming in from Social Security when you retire at age sixty-five, and are able to take $25,000 from your savings. Your adjusted gross income is going to drop to $47,000. If you can put the additional $13,000 into a retirement account each year, you will accomplish two things.

First, you will have an idea about how comfortably you can live off of the income you will have in retirement. Second, adding additional money to your savings will help to increase your financial security in retirement.

There is a final thing to consider regarding how much money you will need in retirement. What additional expenses will you have, once you retire, that you currently do not have? For instance, what about travel and health insurance? If there are additional expenses, figure out how much they will be and simply add that amount to the amount that you put into savings each month. You currently make

$13,000 more per year than you will when you retire.

Now, what you need to do is bring your current, adjusted, gross earnings down to the $47,000 per year number; see if you are able to live off of that amount. If you can, simply put an additional $13,000 into your retirement savings by increasing your contributions by approximately $1,100 per month. If you are not able to make any additional contributions to your retirement savings, make arrangements with your bank to have $1,100 per month moved from your checking account into your savings or investment account.

Once you have your current income adjusted down to what your retirement income will be, try to live on this amount for a full year. The reason to do this for a full year is because we all have different expenses that occur throughout the year. Doing this for a full year will help catch all of these expenses.

If it is very easy, and you have excess money left in your checking account, you will most likely be able to retire and maintain your standard of living. If it is a stretch, but with a little sacrifice you get by, you will probably want to work a little bit longer before you retire. This is because you will have unexpected expenses come up from time to time, like car repairs, house repairs, and medical expenses. If there is no way you could ever live on that amount, then it is better that you found out before you retire than after.

If you do not have enough income to live on, you can either increase your savings or reduce your expenses. One of the best ways to reduce expenses is to pay off all of your debt. Although it is not required to be debt free when you retire, it does reduce your monthly expenses; this will free up some cash each month. If you have $20,000 worth of debt with an 8 percent interest rate, it costs you $1,600 per year just in interest. If this is a ten-year loan, your monthly payment will be around $248 per month. If, instead of having $20,000 in debt, and you had that amount in savings, you could convert that to a stream of income.

This example is for illustration purposes only, and is not a meant as a recommendation. Let's say you put that $20,000 into a fixed annuity in order to receive an income over your lifetime. If you are sixty-five years old and the interest rate is around 4 percent, you would receive about $120 per month. Since you have gone from paying around $248 per month to receiving $120, you have generated additional income by about $4,400 per year. That is a nice increase in income; I think we would all like to obtain additional income like that.

With debt, you are working for your money. With investments, your money is working for you.

Look for other areas that you might want to get under control before you retire. If you gamble on a regular basis, look at how much you lose at the casinos or on lottery tickets. If this is something that you really enjoy, limit your losses. Don't plan on hitting it big, and that will help you retire early. If you think that way, then you probably consider it a high-risk investment. Don't confuse speculation and investment. Investment is where you take some money and invest it in something, expecting a reasonable rate of return. Speculation is where you take some money and put it into something that you hope will give you a huge return. You have to think of gambling as a night out, and take a minimum amount of money to gamble with. When it's gone, you leave.

If you have paid off all of your debt, and feel you have enough saved but still fall short each month, you might need to reduce your spending.

Many of us have a habit of buying things that we see without really thinking about it. Just because something is on sale doesn't mean we need to have it. There have been many techniques that I have read regarding buying stuff. Here is the technique I use for myself when buying things. When you see something you really like, that you think you will get some use out of, don't buy it on the spot.

Compare other prices first to make sure it is a fair price, and then think about how much use you will actually get out of it. If you think you still need it after one week, then you can buy it. This has saved me from buying quite a lot of stuff that I thought I needed, just because it was on sale. Often, after you think about it, you realize you don't really need it. The main thing is to avoid impulse buying, which is where many of us land in trouble.

There is a downside to having a lot of "stuff." Not only does it cost money to buy, but also you need a place to keep it and you need to maintain it. Once you retire you will probably want to do more than maintain a bunch of stuff that you never use or enjoy.

CHAPTER 5
Beware: THINGS THAT CAN DRAIN YOUR SAVINGS

"Money, if it does not bring you happiness, will at least help you be miserable in comfort." —Helen Gurley Brown

The three most common causes I have seen for people running out of money in retirement are gambling, overspending, and children. The reason people are susceptible to this trio when they retire is threefold. They will probably have the largest sum of money at their disposal they have ever had, and once retired you have a lot more time to spend in the stores or at the casinos. Also, if your children know you have just received a large 401(k) rollover, they will be more likely to ask you for financial assistance.

Just like a pack of wild dogs can sense fear, your children can sense when you have money; they might feel they need some of it. Remember, once you retire you probably won't add money to your retirement savings, so what you have in savings is going to have to last. Your adult children should be adding money to their savings, not taking money from you. Don't get me wrong, there might be times when we need to or want to help our children. But, know when to say when.

Okay, here's the last I am going to say about this topic. If you gamble frequently, reduce the amount you allow yourself to lose. If the odds were in your favor at a casino, they couldn't build those big elaborate buildings and offer free drinks.

Unlike real estate or the stock market, where you make money when your investment goes up in value, gambling is an all-or-nothing deal. For someone to make money, someone else needs to lose that exact same amount on every hand played. For example, if you bought a stock at $20 per share, and sold it at $30, you just made $10 per share. No one had to lose that $10 per share for you to be able to make that amount. The person you bought it from might have paid only $10 per share. Real estate is the same way. If you buy a house for $100,000, and sell it for $200,000, you have just made $100,000; no one had to lose $100,000 in order for you to make it. This is because you are investing in an appreciating asset.

When you gamble, if you win $10, that means the casino had to lose $10 in order for you to receive it. You are betting on a zero-sum gain. In other words, no money is created; it just changes hands.

I know a couple that are still working even though they are old enough to retire. They used to max-out their 401(k) and add money to their IRAs each year. They stopped putting money into their IRAs a few years ago, and started to pull money out. I asked them why the sudden change, and they said they had a lot of unexpected expenses. We recently talked, and they confided to me that they were spending more at the casinos. One of their comments was, "We take $50 each, and once that money is gone we're done. This is the same amount we would spend on a nice meal."

The problem with that logic is obvious. First, they wouldn't go out to a nice meal two to four times a week. Second, they started by spending $20 each once a week, and they called this their evening out.

If they were to put the $10,000 per year that they lose at the casinos into an investment that returns 8 percent, after eight years they would have an additional $115,000 in savings. Once again, 8 percent is just an illustration, not an actual investment. If they keep spending the way they currently are, they will need to increase their savings to be able to pay the extra $10,000 per year that they lose at the casinos. That means they probably need to save an additional $200,000 (or more) before they can afford to retire. How long does it take you to save $200,000?

I have another client who retired; she had her house paid off and was debt-free. Between her pension and savings, she was able to make more in retirement than she did working. She called, saying she needed some money to pay off some credit cards. I asked her about the cards, and she explained that she had maxed out her home equity loan as well. I told her that she needed to get her spending under control or she would run out of money. She later confided that she gets bored during the day and likes to go to the casinos for entertainment.

It isn't always the retirees that can spend through their money by gambling; it can be anyone that the retiree trusts with their money.

I have known two widows, their spouses died and left large sums of money, houses, and pensions to them. If you were to look at their financial situation, lifestyles, and assets, you would think there was no way these people could ever run out of money. Both widows didn't know anything about managing these assets, so they both called on their children that they felt were the most qualified to help manage their financial affairs. This is a perfectly logical place to turn when you need help managing something in which you have no knowledge or interest.

In both cases, I knew that the people managing the funds liked to go to the casinos and gamble a little bit. Eventually, in both cases, the children started going to the casinos on a very regular basis. In one case, the markets were doing so well that they were able to take out several thousand dollars per year without their parent noticing it. In the other case, they told their parent that they were taking money from the account to buy other assets. The markets dropped, and the account values started to get very low.

At this point, the type of people who gamble with other people's money think they can gamble more to hit a big score. They both started to gamble more to try to earn back the money they had lost. In both cases, the children had to break it to the parents when all of the money was gone. Although the parents didn't notice their account balances getting close to zero, they did notice when checks bounced or payments from their investment accounts were missed. Once the accounts were depleted, there was no getting them back.

They had to sell the houses; one of these people had a pension and one of them did not. The one who didn't have a pension had only Social Security to live on. At least the other one had her pension left, along with Social Security. Needless to say, the siblings who were counting on that money as their inheritance were not happy with the situation.

In both cases, we often heard about how much the children had won at the casino or on lottery tickets. For people to win consistently at the lottery or at the casinos, they usually have to lose consistently as well. Casinos don't build large elaborate buildings because they pay out more than they take in.

So, be aware. If someone you love is managing your affairs, pay attention to the activity. If you do not understand, ask someone who does to take a look at your accounts from time to time.

Gambling can become very addictive if done on a regular basis; know when to say when. If you think you might have a problem in this area seek out a gambling assistance group before you retire.

In my experience, the second most frequent reason for retired people to run out of money is their kids. This is a tough spot to be in; your child is in trouble and they come to you for help. For most of us, our natural reaction would be to help them out of their situation.

I received a phone call from a good client who was obviously troubled. He said they might need to take a large chunk of money out of their IRA account because their child had gotten into some financial difficulty. It appeared that their child's spouse had developed an addiction of some sort, and was using the money that should have been used to pay household bills to cover the cost of her addiction. Their son found out about this situation when all of the bills started coming in "past due," along with threats of utilities being disconnected and their house being foreclosed. I explained to them that their account had done well, so they had some extra funds they could take if they felt it necessary. But, I also explained that if an emergency was to come up in the future, they might not be able to cover it.

They went to their accountant, and I think the accountant gave them some great advice. "Don't bail them out right away; you have to let them hit rock bottom. If you bail them out too soon, 95 percent will wind up in the same circumstances again."

I don't know if the percentages that he gave are correct, but I do know that what the accountant is saying, in principle, is very true.

I met with a mother and her daughter in my office to go over the mother's financial situation. I wasn't familiar with her family situation and her spending history, so I asked about her outstanding debts, other assets, and income requirements. After getting the whole financial picture, I asked what their major concerns were. The daughter spoke up and said she was concerned that her mother was going to run out of money.

We looked at her mother's withdrawals, and she said, "Mom, you don't have that many expenses; why did you pull out over $50,000 last year?"

After the daughter asked a few questions, the mother finally admitted that she helped her son to the tune of about $30,000. These distributions had two very obvious consequences; they took $30,000 out of her savings and strained the relationship between the daughter and the son. The daughter felt the son was being irresponsible and living beyond his means, using his mother as an ATM. I asked the mother if she had ever bailed her son out before. The daughter rolled her eyes as her mother said, "Only when he really needs help."

There are many stories I could tell you about children draining their parents' life savings, but I hope these few stories will adequately make the point. If your child is in their working years and can't manage their finances now, how are they ever going to be able to manage their finances in the future? If you are always there to help them out when they spend too much, how are they going to learn financial responsibility? What will happen to the children's financial circumstances if they fail to control their spending and you are not around to help them out?

Those are all questions regarding your children's well being, but what about your well being? What happens when you run out of money because you helped out your children? How will they be able to support you if they are not able to support themselves?

If you are going to help an able-bodied child out when they get into financial trouble, only take money from your income, not from your principal. Taking money out of principal is a bad habit to get into, and can cost you your retirement nest egg. Count any money you give your children as a loan, not as a gift. This should have two effects. It will keep a running tab of how much you have given them, and it can cause less strain among the siblings. If you have one responsible and one irresponsible child, it is only reasonable that the responsible child would resent the irresponsible child for draining your life savings.

By helping out a child who does not support himself when he is able, you are becoming an enabler. You are enabling the child to make bad decisions regarding their finances and their lifestyle. You will be better off to let them learn the hard lesson of finances earlier, rather than later.

The third reason I have seen people deplete their retirement savings is overspending. Overspending is not an easy topic to address. You want to enjoy your retirement, and not live out your golden years hoarding like a miser. At the same time, you don't want to spend excessive amounts of money buying things that you don't need and can't afford.

The reason overspending has become such a big issue when we retire, is because we see a big chunk of money in front of us. For most of us, this will be the biggest amount of money we have ever seen. Human nature is to spend it if you have it. So, if you roll over $1,000,000 from your 401(k) you might rationalize that spending $50,000 of that is acceptable. After all, you are only doing it once, and you will still have $950,000 left. You have hardly made a dent in your savings.

But, what you have done is taken one year's worth of income; you've lost the ability for that $50,000 to earn more money. Once it is gone, you can't get it back.

Not only do we have more money now than before, we also have more things to spend it on and more places to spend it. I knew a lady who was very wealthy. When the Home Shopping Network went on the air she began spending all day in front of the TV, waiting for something to come up that she couldn't live without. Her house became stuffed with things that she had bought and had no use for. She did not run out of money, but she spent hundreds of thousands of dollars buying things that she had no use for.

With the advent of the Internet, most of us can sit down in front of our computers and buy almost anything we want, anytime, day or night. Just go to eBay and see if you couldn't buy any sort of luxury item. Whether you are looking for a Rolex, Rolls Royce, mansion, Gucci bag, or a private jet, you can most likely find it there. Some people struggle with spending addictions, and the Internet gives these people another outlet where they can spend their money. Anytime, day or night, during any type of weather, all you need to do is sit down in front of your computer and spend huge amounts of money without even leaving your house.

A good way to reduce spending is to decrease the amount of time you spend in stores, looking at catalogs, and shopping on the Internet. I have a number of hobbies; playing guitar is one of them. I enjoy looking through the catalogs, seeing what type of things they offer that would be nice to have. Each time I look through a guitar catalog, I wind up finding something that I would like to have. Needless to say, there have been times that I would buy something without stopping to think about it first.

If you love to shop, and don't want to give this up, a simple method to reduce your spending is to not buy anything until you have compared prices at four other stores. This works, because it takes so much time; you spend more time shopping and less time buying.

There are many techniques to control spending habits, and many of them work well if you follow them. The secret is finding a method that works well for you. Just like most addictions, we shop because it makes us feel good for a short time. If we do not get it under control, we can increase our debts, decrease our savings, and wind up with a bunch of worthless stuff that we don't even want.

The last thing you want to have happen is to spend through your retirement savings, and have to sell your house and belongings, because you spent too much.

You can learn from my mistakes on this. When I was twenty-one years old, I got hit by a drunk driver and received a $20,000 settlement for my injuries. For a college student in 1987, who was living on $9,000 per year, this was a lot of money. I made a couple of lucky investments, and grew that to almost $30,000. I never made any big purchases. I continued to drive my 1978 Monte Carlo, slept with my mattress on the floor, and ate off of a TV tray. What I started to do was think, "Hey . . . that thing is only $100; I can afford that. I can take some friends out to dinner."

With that, and some over-confident investing, I had drained my savings in four years and was now in deficit spending. I had gotten used to seeing something and just buying it. This is a hard habit to break, and one you do not want to have if you are retired.

If you are married, you and your spouse can hold each other accountable for your purchases. This can give you and your spouse a good opportunity to discuss finances, share ideas, and work on something together. This sounds perfectly logical, but the problem is that many of us don't like to discuss our purchases with our spouse. We want to buy things that they don't want us to buy, and this can cause conflict. The old saying, "It is easier to ask forgiveness than it is to ask permission," is very true when it comes to purchases in most of our marriages.

Although you don't have to use your spouse, they are the best choice. You are both in this together, and when someone has a vested interest, they tend to be more concerned about the outcome.

If you are not married (and maybe even if you are) find some friends and form a group that will hold each other accountable for their spending. We tend to be better behaved when we have to confess our sins (or finances) publicly. This is not an easy thing to do for most people, because we don't want to show our mistakes to anyone.

You can structure this like a book group, where you get together once a month, discuss your purchases, and share ideas about how to save money. It is usually hard for us to talk about personal finances, so you might want to pick some people who you feel comfortable confiding in.

And finally, do not neglect the end-all be-all of financial responsibility. Prepare a budget. A budget is simply a financial diet. For it to work, you need to find a budget that works for you and stick to it. If you start a diet, and then buy a dozen donuts and give into temptation, you are not going to lose weight. If you always give into temptation, you will actually gain weight. If you can't stick to it, you are better off not even being on a diet. Making a budget is the exact same thing. If you don't stick to your spending discipline of a budget, why even have one?

A good way to prepare a budget is to start with all of your fixed expenses. These are the expenses that you will have, no matter what. Add all of your fixed expenses together. For example:

Insurance: $10,000 (health, life, long term care, property, and auto)

Taxes: $7,000 (income and property)

Utilities: $3,000

Food: $6,000

Let's say you have $26,000 in fixed expenses, and you have $50,000 in income. It is a good idea to keep 10 percent for unexpected events, or to underestimate your expenses. After your fixed expenses, and the additional $5,000 cushion for the unexpected, you have $19,000 to spend on clothes, travel, and entertainment. Decide where your priorities are, and allocate an amount to each category.

At the end of the year, review your spending habits. This is very easy to do if you have an account that totals how much you spent where. We opened one of these accounts, and were amazed at how much we spent eating out.

After this review, you can decide where you can spend more or where you should spend less.

No matter what method works best for you to help you keep your spending under control, just remember this one thing. . . .

This is all of the money you have, and once it's gone, it's gone.

CHAPTER 6
Preparing For the Unexpected

"We should all be concerned about the future because we will have to spend the rest of our lives there."

—Charles F. Kettering

It is relatively easy to plan for expected events such as your income needs, activities, lifestyle, and life expectancy. But, how do you prepare for the unexpected?

What will you do if you live to be 110? Don't laugh; go to the Internet and search for 110-year-olds. How many stories will you see? There are a bunch of them. Just fifty years ago, the idea of people living to be 110 was almost unthinkable. Now, it's barely newsworthy. You could spend more time in retirement than you did working.

What happens if you have a very short retirement? According to a study by Ohio State University, the average time spent in retirement in the early twentieth century was three years, now we expect to be retired for fifteen to twenty years. But, there are no guarantees on how many years you will spend in retirement.

What happens if we have economic chaos, high inflation, and a sinking stock market? Will your savings be able to last?

What about if you need assisted care? Can you afford to stay in your home, or do you go to a Medicare facility?

Planning for the most common unexpected events may help prepare you for a long and enjoyable retirement.

I know a guy who had it all planned out; he was going to retire at sixty-two and live off of his Social Security and savings. It worked well for the first two years; then his truck died and he needed to find a replacement. Then, he needed to put a new roof on his house. He simply hadn't planned on these events happening, and was forced to go back to work. These seem like obvious things that he should have planned for, but the idea of being retired was so strong that he was looking at it through rose-colored glasses. When we want something this badly, we tend to be overly optimistic. Fortunately for him, these events occurred when he was fairly young and could easily re-enter the work force. Imagine what it would have been like for him if these events would have occurred ten years after he had retired and was seventy-two years old, instead of just a few years after he was sixty-five?

There are other people who refuse to retire until they are certain that, no matter what happens, they will be financially secure in their retirement. These people tend to work until they die, or come very close to it. The problem with this approach is that no matter how much money you have, you can always see some event that could ruin you financially.

I hate to tell you this, but you cannot possibly be totally covered on every contingency; it is virtually impossible. Think about the people who had planned and were financially secure in Tsarist Russia prior to the revolution, or the people in 1930s Germany prior to Hitler. Outside of keeping substantial assets offshore, and being willing and able to leave for another country on very short notice, there is not a lot you can do about events such as these. Just because events like this can happen doesn't mean you have to plan and prepare for them. You should concentrate on planning for things that are unexpected, but realistically could happen.

Some of these would include long-term-care, a long life, market declines, high inflation, and health care. These are areas that will affect a large number of people in retirement, and thus should be planned for. Major political upheaval only occurs a couple of times a century in the developed world, so I wouldn't spend a lot of time preparing for that.

There needs to be a healthy balance between planning for the unexpected and planning to live. You don't want to retire so early that the slightest unexpected event ruins you financially, and you are forced to come out of retirement. You also don't want to have to work until you are too old to enjoy retirement. You want to have enough to be reasonably assured of a comfortable retirement, with a nice cushion just in case something should occur that you were not expecting.

Being prepared for the unexpected doesn't just mean insurance. It also means wills and trusts, having your assets organized so that if something were to happen to you, your heirs or beneficiaries could utilize the assets. Making sure that objects are titled correctly, and beneficiaries are clearly established, is a good start.

You might wonder why it is important for you to get your affairs in order before you retire. It is simple. If you become disabled or incapacitated you will want your assets to be able to provide for your care, even though you are not able to direct them anymore. When you die, you would want your assets to provide for your surviving spouse or be distributed according to your wishes. If you leave your estate in a shambles your assets might still get distributed the way you wanted, but there is a chance they wouldn't be. If your assets are disorganized, and you have no clear instructions regarding how to handle your estate, it will be much more difficult for your spouse and heirs to access these assets. If you become disabled, and are no longer able to take care of your own financial matters, you will want someone you trust to do this for you. If you leave this to chance it may take a longer period of time, and cost much more, than if you had done a little planning and preparation in advance. There is also the matter of who will handle your financial matters if you become incapacitated. Do you want a complete stranger, or a family member that you don't trust, handling your financial affairs? A little planning could save a lot of headaches down the road, not just for you but also for your spouse and heirs.

Let's start with the easiest and most important things to do. I know this sounds morbid, and many people don't want to talk about it, but you should have a "When I die" folder. I know it would be easier to say an "In case I die" folder, and while I hate to break it to you, death is inevitable. Everybody dies, and we never know when, so it is better to prepare in advance.

What's a "When I die" folder, you ask? It is simply a folder that lists your assets, insurance policies, bank accounts, and other assets and holdings. It also holds your trusts, wills, powers of attorney, and other legal documents. It tells the location of these items, and who your heirs should contact to get these items taken care of. This will give you peace of mind in knowing that many of your affairs are in order. I work with a county administrator on both custodial issues and estate distributions, so I have seen what it is like to work with a poorly planned estate. Not only does it help you in case you should become incapacitated, it can also help avoid family conflict after you are gone.

One estate I helped settle involved a couple that both passed on within a year of each other, which is not that unusual an occurrence. This couple had collected objects over the years from their travels, and some of the pieces were quite valuable. They hadn't listed what went to whom, so when their children went through the house they agreed that each child could pick one item that they wanted. After each child picked their object, then each grandchild could pick an item. Once this was agreed, one of the children went over and picked up the Lalique figure from a table. They had estimated the value of the piece at about $75,000. The other children had no idea of the value, but could tell by this person's action that this piece had substantial value. I guess the child that chose the Lalique figure was aware of the value of this piece prior to making the selection.

Since the piece had by far the highest appraised value, this caused a bit of a feud within the family. The child's siblings started feeling that she just wanted the most expensive thing, and didn't care about sentimental value.

In the "When I die" folder, you can label your most valued possessions and designate who they should go to when you pass on. You can also give a brief explanation as to why you are selecting this person for that object. They will appreciate it, and it might help the family relationship after you are gone. Unless your explanation is, "Because you are my favorite, and I never cared for any of the others that much," your heirs will enjoy hearing the sentimental value you had for a particular object.

In the "When I die" file, you'll want to list the location of your accounts, insurance policies, land, any other assets you will be passing on. Make a copy of the file and give it to someone you trust, and keep a copy for yourself. This way, when you are gone, the people handling your estate will be able to manage your affairs more easily. It ensures that the people you wanted to be able to use the money can use it in a timely fashion.

You wouldn't believe some of the stuff we have had to deal with in trying to settle some people's affair after they have passed on.

One case was particularly interesting. A guy passed on with no clear heirs, no will, and investments scattered all over the place. He had bank accounts, stock certificates, brokerage accounts, land, and a few collectibles. The administrator of his estate went through his house and gathered up all of his financial papers. He brought me an orange box. I don't mean its color was orange; I mean it was one of those big boxes that oranges come in. It was stuffed to overflowing with statements, bonds, stock certificates, and dividend checks. Yes, that's right . . . dividend checks. They were just sitting there; they hadn't been cashed and many of them were over a year old. I don't know if he misplaced them, forgot about them, or just didn't want to hassle with cashing them, but there they were. After several hours, we finally got everything sorted out. Or, at least we got everything organized that we could find. We opened a single account, and started to deposit all of these items into this account. Once this was done, I prepared a date of death valuation for estate tax purposes. A few statements would trickle in from time to time, showing he had additional assets that we were not aware of, and we would transfer those into the central account. After two years we received a dividend check from a phone company. I contacted them, and they said he still had seven hundred shares of their stock worth about $28,000. I don't know about you, but that is a lot of money to misplace. There were no certificates to be found, and so we had to apply for a lost certificate. This cost over $1,500, and delayed the distribution of the estate by several months.

After all was said and done, he had about $900,000 after taxes, fees, and paying off all of his funeral expenses. The administrator tracked down his closest heirs . . . two nieces. No one knew if he liked them, or if they even knew he existed. But, since he had not stated anything to the contrary before he died, the courts decided who should get his money. The nieces were summoned into court. They showed up and each received a check for over $450,000. Now that's a pleasant surprise.

Whether he wanted the money to go to his nieces didn't matter, because he didn't leave any instructions. If you don't decide where your money should go, somebody else will.

A big part of organizing your assets is to not hold stock and bond certificates. By holding stocks and bonds in certificate form, you have to keep track of the certificates, deposit the dividend checks, and keep current with mergers, acquisitions, and name changes.

My father held Sears stock; he kept certificates in various places around the house. Sears spun off Allstate and Dean Witter, and then Kmart bought Sears. You could either take the new Sears holding stock or receive $50 cash per share. Since my dad had his shares in certificate form, and never contacted the transfer agent (a transfer agent is a company that holds and administers your stock certificates) the stocks were converted to the $50 per share. It has been almost four years since my father passed away and we still have some shares that we are trying to cash in, along with a certificate that we cannot find. This has cost us substantial dollars in a couple of ways. First off, if the Sears shares had been converted like my father wanted, the shares would have been worth over $100 per share instead of the $50 that they were cashed in for. The second reason is that, if we could have taken the $50 per share and put it into a bank CD paying 4 percent over the past four years, we would have over 16 percent more funds than we do now. If Dad had kept these stock certificates in a brokerage account, it would have been much easier to convert to the new shares. Even if he hadn't converted these shares, the $50 per share proceeds would have gone directly into a money market account, and could have at least earned some interest while we were sorting everything out.

If you hold stock and bond certificates, please just open a brokerage account and consolidate your shares into a single account if possible.

Here are a few of the advantages of consolidating your stocks in one account:

1. Consolidates your asset so you can keep track of them better.
2. Keeps your certificates so you don't have to worry about where they are.

3. Lets you easily convert your shares in case of a merger or acquisition.
4. Puts proceeds and dividends into a money market immediately so you earn more interest.
5. Some accounts will track cost basis and dividend reinvestment on your shares.
6. You can access via a debit card or check writing.
7. It is easier to track your portfolio value and income generated by your portfolio.
8. In most states, a consolidated account can be set up as a trust, transfer on death or joint tenant with right of survivor, so your beneficiaries can avoid probate.

The potential downside that some people will mention is that these accounts usually have a cost associated with them. Most brokerage firms will charge anywhere from $25 to $200 per year to hold your certificates and other investments. Some will not charge anything if there is activity in the account. What do you pay each year for a safe deposit box? If you own enough stock certificates, an account that costs $50 per year to maintain might well be worth the cost.

I just had a client who owned a stock that got bought out by another company. The stock had split several times since she had owned it, so she had numerous certificates. When she had to send in the certificates to receive her money, she discovered she did not have one of the certificates. We had to send in a check for over $2,700 to replace those lost certificates. That is a lot of money to part with just for a piece of paper.

Some people don't want a broker calling them trying to buy or sell investments. If you are that type of person, you can open an account at a discount brokerage firm that doesn't make such calls.

The stocks you keep in a brokerage account are protected in a similar way to the money you keep in the bank. If the firm fails, the Securities Investors Protection Corporation (SIPC) offers protection up to $500,000 per firm per investor. Some firms will carry additional securities account protection through the Customer Asset Protection Company (CAPCO). This protection does not cover market losses (when your account loses value because of a drop in asset value) or fraud by the firm or the broker. It only covers your account, subject to certain conditions & limitations, in case the firm fails.

Although SIPC does not guarantee your account against loss from fraud or unauthorized trading, there are other safeguards against that type of activity. The firm that holds your account is responsible for proper supervision of its registered representatives. If one of their brokers is handling your account in an illegal or unethical manner, that brokerage firm should be responsible for their representative's actions.

A good way to protect yourself from placing your investments in a company that might go bankrupt is to look at the credit rating of the brokerage firm you are considering. Generally, the scale rates companies from AAA to C or D. In these ratings, AAA is the highest and D means default. Companies such as Standard and Poor's and Moody's provide these ratings. These rating agencies assess the probability of the brokerage firms going bankrupt. The higher the rating (AAA being the highest) the more secure the rating agency feels the company is. This doesn't mean a AAA company can't fail; it just means someone has done research on that company and feels it is very unlikely that it would fail.

Many brokerage firms hold their assets in trust at other firms. In other words, a brokerage firm might execute trades and generate statements and confirmations, but they do not actually hold the assets. They could be held at another bank or brokerage firm. In this case, it is more important to know the rating of the institution that is holding the assets. Finding out who will hold the assets is very easy; just ask the representative who their clearing firm is and who holds the assets. You are then able to go to the library, or go online, to see how these firms are rated.

The type of brokerage firm you open an account with can make a big difference. It has been my experience that most companies either encourage activity in the accounts or charge a fee for service. If you have been investing on your own, do not feel you need the assistance of a broker, and like the Internet, you can open an account and manage it online. If you do go with an individual broker, make sure they are licensed to handle your stocks and bonds and have an adequate amount of experience.

To find out about a prospective broker's history, I recommend a broker search on http://www.finra.org, the Financial Industry Regulatory Authority's Web site. You can look to see what licenses the broker holds, how long they have been in the business, and if they have any registered complaints against them. This website does not rate the competency or quality of a broker's services, but it can help you learn about this person's history as a broker.

There are several things you need to be aware of when investing. Beware of frauds and schemes! You have worked too hard for your money to see it vanish through a Ponzi scheme or other illegitimate investment.

1. Ask for online access to your account.
2. Make sure the statements are legitimate.
3. See if the firm has a parent company to back it up in case there is trouble.
4. Find out who audits the firm and look at the annual statements.
5. Only rely on audited performance results.
6. If someone is performing well when everyone else is not, that could be reason for concern.

Once you have your affairs in order, it is time to plan for the things you hope won't happen, but might.

Let's talk about what happens if you are unable to take care of yourself. At the point in time when you need long-term care, you will not be able to go back to work to help pay for it. Basically, you will have three options. You can have a family member or loved one take care of you, use your assets or private insurance to pay for long-term care services, or get rid of all of your assets and check into a Medicaid facility. A tricky thing about Medicaid is the five-year-look-back. If you give your assets away in order to qualify for Medicaid, Medicaid can audit you up to five years. If you qualify for Medicaid because you gave your assets away, Medicaid might require you to wait for services or require that the assets be returned. Please consult someone who is knowledgeable about Medicaid before doing any planning of asset distributions.

According to *Long Term Care* at www.ltc-usa.com, it is estimated that over 65 percent of seniors will need some type of long-term care during their lifetime. For people whose circumstances have necessitated a move into an assisted living facility, the average stay has been about three years. According to the MetLife Mature Market Institute's study, the average annual cost of an assisted living facility is $36,372, or $77,380 for a private room in a nursing home. Large cities tend to be higher priced on average, and rural areas tend to be lower priced, but regardless of where you live, it is not cheap.

Receiving long-term care can be a tricky business if you do not have insurance or adequate assets to pay for it. If you are unable to pay for your long-term care, you can have a family member take care of you. It will usually be a child, and in my experience in this matter, it is often a daughter who provides the care. If this is not an option, you can spend down all of your assets so you can be eligible to go into a Medicaid room at an assisted living facility. This option may not be available in all states. If you are planning on the Medicaid room, you will want to plan in advance; many assisted living facilities have long waiting lists for their Medicaid rooms.

Since neither of these are a particularly good alternative I would suggest private insurance or a large amount of assets. Most people will be unable to accumulate a substantial amount of assets to pay for long-term care on their own, so long-term care insurance is probably a better option.

Long-term care insurance can be oversold, but more often than not, in my opinion, it is the most undersold insurance there is.

Here is a situation where it is oversold; consider the case of individuals with substantial assets and very large or multiple homes. The cost to keep up these houses could easily exceed the cost of an assisted living facility. If you are living alone when you need to move into an assisted living facility, you will no longer need your house. In most cases, you would sell your house because you no longer have a need for it. This would rid you of that expense, and provide assets for you to live on. Depending on the size and maintenance cost of the house, you might not be spending that much more to live in an assisted living facility than you did when you were living in your house.

For example, say you own a house where you live alone. Your total living expenses to stay in this house are $48,000 per year. Each month you spend $4,000 on transportation, food, taxes, heating, cooling, and maintenance. Once you go into a nursing home you will no longer need that house, and most likely will dispose of it by selling it or giving it to your children. Let's say the facility you have just checked into costs $77,380 per year; this is the average cost of a private room in a nursing home in 2008. Some agents may attempt to sell you long-term care insurance by saying, "Your current expenses are $48,000 per year, and a nursing home will run you about $77,000 per year, so you are going to need $125,000 per year just to cover your expenses. Can you afford almost $325 per day to cover your bills?"

This high, daily amount of income is only needed if you will keep the house. In fact, most people in that situation will not keep a house they are not living in. So, in this example, your expenses will be only the cost of the nursing home. Since you are selling the house and virtually doing away with most of your other expenses, you have gone from $48,000 per year to around $77,380 per year. You will need to be able to make up a difference of $29,380 per year (the difference between your current expense and the nursing home cost).

The example above is relevant if you are single or living alone. If you are a couple, and live in a house together, you might have the situation where one of you needs skilled nursing care and the other does not. This situation is when long-term care insurance becomes valuable. If you do not have long-term care insurance, or substantial assets to cover both the cost of a nursing home, and to maintain a house, you have a tough choice to make. Do you maintain a house and a room in a nursing home, depleting your assets until there is nothing left, or do your spouse or children become caregivers and take care of you?

In most situations, having the care provided at home by a professional caregiver is usually preferred. You don't have to leave your home and you don't have to spend a lot of time shopping for the best nursing home. Many people do not want to become a burden on their children, so they would rather have a professional caregiver come into their house to clean, care for them, and dress them.

Here is an example. Imagine a couple in their nineties, living in a large home. They have two children who are both retired. The mother needs long-term care, and the father, being in his nineties, can get along on his own but is unable to take care of her. One child visits their parents regularly and takes care of the mother, while the other child visits occasionally. The burden becomes too much for the husband and child to handle, so they hire a full-time caregiver. The combined cost of the caregiver and the cost of the house start to eat away at their assets. After a couple of years of maintaining the house, and paying for full-time caregivers, they are rapidly running out of money. They decide to sell the house and move Mom into an assisted living facility; they also move Dad into a small apartment close to his wife. If the parents pass on while there are any assets left, they will leave what's left of the estate to their children. If they run out of assets while they are both still alive, how would they pay for the father's living expenses? We know that the mother can go into a Medicaid room at some facility, but how will the father support himself?

In this example, long-term care insurance could have helped alleviate much of the financial burden, as well as emotional and financial stress. Some long-term care policies allow for compensation to family members who take care of the person that qualifies for assisted care.

It might not seem like anything to get worried about, but in this example you have one child who does all of the care giving. Yet, if there are any assets left, each of the children will receive the same amount. If there was insurance to pay for the caregiver, they might not have had to sell the house. The parents might have been able to stay in the surroundings in which they were comfortable for the remainder of their days.

Since this couple didn't have enough assets to maintain their house and pay for long-term care, they needed to make dramatic changes to their lifestyles. The child who took care of the parents probably did not receive any compensation for her efforts, even though those efforts enabled the estate to be much larger than it otherwise would have been. The house was sold to cover current expenses, and the amount of money left to the children was substantially less.

If there were only one parent living who needed long-term care, the issue would have been much easier to deal with. When you have two parents managing this situation, it is much more difficult, especially if no planning has been done in advance.

Most of us know, or have known, people who needed long-term

care because they were no longer able to care for themselves. The one I am most familiar with was my grandmother. She was in her nineties when she sold her home and moved into an assisted living facility. It was an amazing experience. She had lost much of her mobility and didn't feel she could continue to maintain her house. She was unhappy about having to move into an assisted living facility. After she moved into her new apartment, she began to get settled in. Her new apartment had a great view and offered activities. She began meeting new friends and just having a good old time. Her mind became sharper and she was back to being her cheery self. After a couple of years at this assisted living facility, she fell and hit her head. Although she was still mentally alert, her health began to decline. My mother and aunt were faced with the situation of moving her to a nursing home, or hiring a nursing staff to take care of her. They chose to hire a nursing staff. This added much time and enjoyment to my grandmother's life. It was a burden on my mother, making sure there was always someone there to take care of my grandmother when needed. My grandmother was not a rich woman, but she did have a pension and the proceeds from the sale of her house to help cover the costs of the at-home care she received.

The other situation I came across was an elderly couple, both in their nineties. The husband had a stroke and was bound to a wheelchair. Although he was not able to get around without his wheelchair, he was still very sharp mentally. This couple had substantial assets and wanted to stay in the big house they had lived in for over fifty years. One day, when the wife was helping her husband into the wheelchair, she fell, bumped her head, and broke her hip. This caused her to be confined to a wheelchair as well. The children decided they would hire people to help provide at-home care so their parents could live out their lives in the home in which they raised their children. Both the husband and wife lived for many years after being confined to wheelchairs. After some time, they began to spend through most of their assets. If they would have had to pay the nursing service for their entire lives, they might have run out of money. Fortunately, they had a daughter who took on the responsibility of managing the caregivers. This was a burden on the daughter, but she was happy that her parents could spend their final years in the home where she grew up.

The reason why I wanted to talk about long-term care in a book about retirement is that I want you to have a long, happy retirement. It is something that we don't like to think about, but it is a very real possibility. According to a Wall Street Journal study published on February 25, 2007, there is a 70 percent chance that one member of a couple will need long-term care. The two examples I gave regarding long-term care were both couples in their nineties, but I have seen people in their fifties, sixties, seventies, and eighties need long-term care. One thing I want you to avoid is a situation where you work all of your life to retire with the one you love, only to realize that they need some sort of long-term care shortly after you retire. Without the proper planning, you could deplete your retirement savings by taking care of them. If this is a permanent disability, you will need to take care of them for the remainder of their lives. You now have lost the love of your life while you are still fairly young, and you don't have the retirement savings you had planned on.

If you have not looked into buying long-term care insurance, you should see if it is appropriate for you. Find an adviser who is familiar with LTC insurance who can customize a policy to fit your needs and your budget. Don't just buy the cheapest long-term care insurance (LTCI) policy because even though you are saving money, you might not get the coverage you need. Also, don't just call your insurance agent and say, "I need long-term care insurance. Can you help me?" Get a couple of quotes from people who specialize in LTCI and can explain the advantages and disadvantages of each policy, along with features and benefits that you might want or need.

Long-term care insurance is like any type of insurance; if you need it, it can easily pay for itself. If you never need it, you have spent a lot of money. I would argue that, even if you don't need it, you have not wasted your money; you have given yourself some protection and peace of mind. You don't see people saying," My house never burned down so I wasted all that money on homeowners insurance," or "I never wrecked my car so auto insurance was a waste." Don't feel bad if you were able to provide protection for you and your family and never used it.

One very important thing about LTCI is that, if you pay for it, you want it to be there if and when you need it. It is important that you understand what your policy will and won't cover. It is also important that your insurance company will still be around to pay for those expenses if they were to occur. Although there is no guarantee that any one insurance company will be around in ten, twenty or fifty years, you should look at a company that has been around for a while and has a good financial rating from the major financial ratings services. These services include AM Best, Moody's, Standard and Poor's, and Duff and Phelps.

Even though there is a 60 percent chance that you individually will need long-term care at sometime in your life, there is a 100 percent certainty that you will die. Hopefully it will be many years down the road, and you will have had a long and enjoyable retirement.

Have you planned for your loved ones in case you should pass on before them? Most of the insurance agents I know will tell you why you need more life insurance. They might be right, but I wouldn't recommend buying more insurance than you can afford. What I would recommend is that you consider how much income your spouse will lose if you should go before him/her. Ask yourself these questions:

1. Do I have a pension that goes away when I do?
2. Does my spouse have his/her own Social Security?
3. What expenses go away when I pass on?
4. Do we have adequate savings to provide the income needed?

Many people only think about replacement of income if they are working, but in many cases income needs to be protected in retirement as well.

In most cases, the household expenses will go down when there is only one person living in that household, but there are situations where they might actually increase.

Let's say you do all of the yard work, home maintenance, and minor auto repair. You cook, clean the house, and shop for all of the household items that are needed. If your spouse is unable or unwilling to do this, especially if you are not around, they will have to hire someone. That will cost money; it might even cost more than your expenses did.

To prepare for this possible circumstance, look at how much your spouse does around the house. Determine who you would need to hire if they should pass on. If you don't have any idea, call a handyman, lawn-care company, or a housekeeping service that you might hire if that time came. Try to figure how often they would need to do their thing, and put an annual cost to it. For example, if you clean out the gutters five times a year, mow the grass weekly and trim the hedges once a year, get a quote.

Let's say gutter cleaning costs $100; five times a year equals $500. Run down the list of items and total it up. Then, look at the expenses that are directly related to your spouse. Figure in roughly half of the food bill, any insurance or fees, and club dues, or memberships. If he/she has a car that will be sold or given away, add that expense to the list.

Once you have everything you can think of pulled together, add them up to see how much income will go away, versus how much your expenses will go up or down.

Here is how this works:

Lost income is:

Pension will go from $1,800 per month to $900 per month.

Social Security of $1,600 per month will go away.

Total loss of income is $2,500 per month, or $30,000 per year.

Decreased expenses are:

Car payments, upkeep, and taxes are $2,400 per year.

Food and living expenses of $6,700 per year will be reduced to $3,350.

Memberships, clubs, and hobbies will be reduced by $3,300.

The total decrease in expenses is $9,050.

Cost to replace the services you provide:

Gutter cleaning, yard work, and other items are $2,400 per year.

Now that you have an idea of the loss of income, combined with the loss of service and decreased expenses, you can see how much annual income you need to be able to replace. In this example, it would be $30,000 of annual income minus the $9,050 in annual expense reduction, plus $2,400 to replace the services. So, the total annual shortfall to their income is going to be around $22,450. If you have adequate assets to offset this drop in income, then you need not worry about additional life insurance. Many insurance agents would now argue that you would still need the insurance to pay expenses and estate taxes, but that is not the purpose of this book. The purpose of this book is to help you retire comfortably and stay retired, not how to leave more money for your heirs. That topic is better suited for a different book.

If you currently do not have the assets to replace that type of income, life insurance is one of the most effective ways to deliver those assets to replace the loss.

Using the example above, with the annual decrease of $23,050, per year, how much life insurance will you need to replace that amount of income? It will depend on several factors; how long will you live and what activities you want to do are two of the major considerations. The younger you are, and the more things you want to do, the amount of insurance will typically be higher. The old rule of thumb was eight times the amount of income you want to replace. In this example, that would be $184,400. That amount might be too much or too little depending on your circumstances, but it would be better than having nothing at all to replace the lost income.

You have insurance on your car and you have insurance on your house. Don't you think it's a good idea to have insurance on you?

The reason we buy insurance is to protect against loss. When we are younger and we have a loss, we are able to work a little longer to recover from that loss. Once you are retired, these losses could force you to go back to work, or dramatically reduce your standard of living.

There is a final item on preparing for the unexpected. If you are currently handling all of the finances for someone else, whether it is your spouse, child, sibling, or friend, get them involved in the finances, especially if you do your own investing and prepare all of the taxes. Many times I have seen someone lose their spouse after many years of marriage, and the surviving spouse has never done anything with the finances. This is a very bad situation because they are grieving a loss, not thinking rationally, and now they have to deal with something they are unfamiliar with. It can be very difficult getting the other person to take an interest in your finances if they do not want to get involved. But it is very important to at least introduce them to someone you would trust, to help them out, if you were to pass on before them. I have seen it happen with my clients where one spouse handles the finances and tries to get their spouse to take an interest. It is not always the husband who handles the finances; I have seen many times where it is the wife.

Usually, it will happen something like this. A couple will come into my office, and one of them will try to get the other one more informed about their finances. The one who handles the finances will try to explain something to the other, and they have no interest in learning anything about it.

If you are in this situation, and you are handling the finances for someone else and they will not take an interest in what is going on, please have a trusted advisor that they can turn to if you should check out before them. Do a little research so you have some level of confidence that they are actually honest and trustworthy.

Through my investment advisory business, I have seen many people who have portfolios that were not appropriate for them. Some paid no fees at all, some paid very high fees, and some were paying twice and didn't even realize it. I have seen people paying over 2 percent in management fees who had sub-par performance; I have seen people who paid next to nothing and received great service and performance. Just because you pay a lot doesn't mean that you will get a lot. Just because you don't pay a lot doesn't mean you will get bad service. Just be careful not to be impressed with a big office and a fancy title.

Titles and designations do not mean that someone will be a trusted advisor. Remember that a title of vice president does not mean that this person is an investment guru; this title is usual given to people who generate a certain level of commission or fees for their firm.

Designations such as, chartered financial analyst, chartered financial consultant, and the Certified Financial Planner certification, mean that this person has been through some type of training and testing above and beyond just getting a securities license. A designation usually illustrates that the people who possess these designations and certifications have made a conscious effort to expand their knowledge. If they have a designation it can be viewed as a plus, but it still is no guarantee that they will be a good advisor. Many people use titles and designations like a drunk uses a lamppost, for support rather than illumination. Even though a designation is a good thing to have, they are not the only things to consider when choosing an advisor.

When checking out a prospective advisor, please do not think that titles or designations are the only things worth considering. Look at their experience, expenses, and method of advisory. When selecting an advisor, make sure you are comfortable with what they have to say and the products that they recommend.

If the adviser you are interviewing becomes agitated because you are asking questions, talks down to you, or changes the subject when you ask tough questions, they might not be a good fit.

Up to now, we have covered things that can happen to you. Now, we will get into what can happen to the market, interest rates, and the economy.

Investment decisions can cause you to lose your life savings. This usually happens when someone is investing too aggressively and they are not able to withstand a long, steep drop in their investments. Also, they might have a concentrated position in one investment. The closer you are to retirement, the more important it is to have a well-diversified portfolio.

No one knows when the market is going to go up significantly, and no one knows when it is going to go down. If someone could predict the movement of the market, they could have more money than Warren Buffett.

To me, the most amazing thing about the market is that when more people invest a certain way, the more likely it is that a certain type of investment will be overvalued. I am not just talking about the stock market. I am talking about any market where people invest their money. You might have heard that famous line from Joe Kennedy about how the time to get out of the market is when you get a stock tip from your shoeshine boy. This means that everyone who can possibly put their money into this investment already has their money in it, so there is nothing left to push the price up higher. Once an investment cannot go up any further, it will likely go down. We saw this happen in the late 1990s with tech stocks, and in 2006 with the real estate market. The problem is that there is no guarantee that it will go down just because everyone is talking about it. But, it usually is a pretty good indicator.

One of the all-time great investors, Sir John Templeton, said, "Bull markets are born in pessimism, mature in optimism, and die in euphoria." In other words, usually the best time to buy is when most people are telling you to sell, and usually the best time to sell is when everyone is telling you to buy.

Be very skeptical of someone who promises you high returns with little or no risk. Most of the investment systems I have seen do not provide above-market returns. If somebody figures out a system that will out-perform the market consistently, with little or no risk, don't you think the people who invented it would make a great living using their own systems, rather than running around the country trying to get you to buy it?

There are market timing services that charge fees to tell you when to get in or out of the market, in an attempt to buy low and sell high on a short-term basis. However, this strategy can be extremely risky and may not be for the everyday investor. I have yet to see any research that shows any of these market timing services outperforming the market on the long-term.

The question still remains on how you should invest for retirement. I will give you a couple of ideas, but retirement is unique to each person who experiences it. Thus, I am not able to give you specifics of how you should invest your money.

The biggest concern you will have is buying risk; what can you buy with the money you have? If your investments go down you cannot buy as much. If inflation goes up and your investments stay the same, you cannot buy as much. If interest rates go down and you depend on your interest-paying investments to live on, you cannot buy as much. So, how do you protect yourself against these types of risks?

Unless you have a large enough portfolio to allow you to reinvest your interest to keep pace with inflation, you will need to invest some of your portfolio in assets that historically have substantially outperformed the rate of inflation. These investments are usually stocks, natural resources, real –estate, or inflation-indexed bonds.

To help protect against a drop in interest rates, there are a couple of products that you can utilize. You can invest in long-term bonds with call protection, or purchase an immediate annuity. A long-term bond is a bond with at least fifteen years to maturity; a call feature allows the issuer to redeem the bond before the maturity date if the interest rates have decreased. An immediate annuity is a contract purchased with a single payment that is converted to a steady stream of income that lasts a lifetime (or a specified number of years). Some options let you pass payments on to a beneficiary after you're gone.

To protect against rising interest rates, you can invest in short-term bonds. When you invest in short-term bonds, you have bonds that will mature within a year or two. If interest rates rise, you can then reinvest these bond proceeds into a higher yielding bond. If you were to buy long-term bonds when interest rates are low, there is the risk that rates will rise and the value of your current bonds will decrease.

You should plan an allocation that incorporates many of these items; this will help protect against the uncertainty of investing in any one type of investment.

Some people think that short-term certificates of deposit are the safest things to invest in. But, after you pay taxes and factor in inflation, you may not be allowing yourself to maintain your buying power; the interest rates paid on these short-term C/Ds may not keep up with inflation. When interest rates dropped in the early nineties and the early two thousands, people who had all of their investments in short-term bonds and C/Ds saw their income drop, in some cases by as much a 60 percent.

Every investment has its risks; you need to have an appropriate allocation of different types of investments to manage these risks.

Now that we have dealt with the unexpected things that can happen once you retire, let's get into some things that can help you have a longer, happier retirement.

CHAPTER 7
Don't Get Overwhelmed

"The individual has always had to struggle to keep from being overwhelmed by the tribe. To be your own man is a hard business. If you try it, you will be lonely often, and sometimes frightened. But no price is too high to pay for the privilege of owning yourself."

—Rudyard Kipling

My father was noted for not finishing things. He had more half-finished projects than you can imagine. This is how it happened. My father had seven children; when I was two years old he bought the farm that has been in the family since 1846. The thing about a farm is that there is always something that needs to be done. Just imagine if your yard was 111 acres and you needed it to always look good. It started off well enough . . . some roofs needed mending, some fences needed fixing, and the cows needed milking. No matter what the circumstances, the cows always need milking, twice a day no matter what the temperature was. After several years of living on the farm, a few new projects started. So, now not only were there the regular farm chores to do, but my dad decided we needed to put an addition to the house, put a new engine in the red pickup truck, and build a tack shed to store all of our saddles, bridles, and what not. Every time something would need fixing, it got put on the "to-do" list. Every time a new project was started. it also went on the "to do" list.

This all seems like a perfectly logical approach to managing tasks, but there was one flaw in the system; you need to finish one task before you start another. So, what happened? We wound up with more projects than could be completed and we became overwhelmed.

You would walk out of the front door, which also needed repair, and all you could see were things that needed to be done. It was overwhelming; you didn't know where to begin because there was so much to do. Since tasks seldom were finished, things just continued to pile up and there was no end in sight. There was no hope of ever catching up on all of the things that needed to get done.

Once my father had fallen that far behind it was no longer a matter of preventative maintenance, it had become crisis management. The gutters had rotted through and should have been replaced. This never got done because it was way down on the "to do" list. By the way, there was never an actual list; it was just things that obviously needed to be done.

The reason for gutters is to keep water away from the foundation of the house. After a few years the foundation to the house started to crumble, and we had to put supports under the house to keep it from falling in. I am not making this up; you can call my mother and ask her if you would like. Do I need to tell you what happens to a house when the foundation starts to crumble?

Sometimes a little prevention goes a long way. Whether it is your car, house, or body, a little preventative work can save a lot of time and money in the long run.

When you get in a situation where it seems that you have no chance of ever getting caught up, it wears you out both physically and mentally. You see what needs to be done, you become overwhelmed, and then you go take a nap. When you get to this point you no longer work on what you had planned to work on, and you start to neglect the things that really need to get done.

We have all experienced this sensation at one point or another in our lives. You are confronted with what appears to be an insurmountable obstacle and you slouch down and say to yourself, "How in the world am I ever going to finish that?" The answer is that you may not be able to finish that big project.

I have some of the same tendencies that my father had; I would take on more projects than I could finish. My wife finally put it to me in a way that made sense.

"So, what hobbies are you willing to give up in order to finish that car?"

After some thought, the answer was "none."

I had purchased the car a couple of years before we were married. It was a 1966 Ford Thunderbird with a 429 engine, yellow with a black top. It really was a good-looking car. I had taken it to a body shop and had the body rebuilt from the ground up. This car was a hard-top, which wasn't what I really wanted; what I really wanted was a convertible. I had settled for this car because the convertibles were out of my price range. The fact of the matter was that it was not the perfect car for us, and therefore it wasn't a priority for me to finish.

Every time I would look at that car I felt bad about not making any progress. I sold the car and took a loss on it, and never again had to feel bad every time I walked into the garage. I learned a valuable lesson; when you have more important things to do, don't spend your time and money on things that are not high on your priority list.

A simple strategy to combat the tendency to over-commit ourselves is to make a list of everything you want to get done, both before and after you retire. If you are anything like me, you will be amazed by the amount of stuff you have on the list. I looked at all of the things that I wanted to accomplish. These items ranged from fixing up the Thunderbird to working on the house, to writing this book (since you are reading it I obviously finished that one) to having some quiet time each day. The final list was over two hundred items long.

I showed the list to my wife and she quickly prioritized the items most important to her. These were ten items that she wanted finished sooner rather than later, and most involved work to the house or things that would benefit the family.

When I saw a list of over two hundred items, I realized they were not small tasks; some would take hundreds of hours to complete. I quickly realized that I had bitten off more than I could chew. It was time to see what items were important enough to work on, and which ones needed to hit the proverbial scrap heap.

Prior to doing this exercise, I would look at all of the projects around me and just get exhausted thinking about all of the things I needed to do. After completing this little exercise, I was able to start working on the things that were the most important things that I needed to get done in my life. Immediately, I felt so much better about myself and my accomplishments; my energy level went way up and I started sleeping better at night.

The reason for this chapter is to reinforce the importance of prioritization. If you do not have priorities, then you might wind up doing some things that are not that important, while the things that matter more to you get neglected.

So, before you retire, I would recommend that you get all of those nagging tasks that you have been meaning to do for years, out of your life. Either finish them or get rid of them.

CHAPTER 8
Retirement on Your Terms

"Retirement is waking up in the morning with nothing to do and by bedtime having done only half of it." —Author Unknown

When you come to your final days, will you have regrets about how you spent your life? Many people do. I have seen a couple of different surveys of residents of nursing homes; the studies questioned what regrets these people had about the way they lived their lives. The results showed that the major regrets these people had in their later years were not spending more time with family, not traveling or doing things they wanted to do, and not taking more hot baths. Many regretted putting their work before their family and friends. And, many regretted not taking more risks or opportunities.

Few people live without regrets as to how they could have spent their lives better. Hopefully, your joys will be greater than your regrets. This is why it is so important to figure out what is most important to you in your life, so you can accomplish great things in your retirement. When you retire, it is your life and the lives of the people you care about that should be most important to you. Set priorities and enjoy it; you only live once.

One thing to avoid is getting bogged down with activities that you do not want to do, or that you don't need to do.

We have all had this happen before; someone calls you to do something you really aren't that interested in doing. You don't have anything better to do, so you agree to join this person in whatever task it is. After you are already committed, a much better offer comes up for the same time as the thing you didn't really want to do in the first place. Now, you have passed up something you really wanted to do because you agreed to do something you really didn't want to do, and you wind up kicking yourself for agreeing to do something you didn't really want to do.

When you were doing the thing you didn't want to do in the first place, were you a little resentful of the person who invited you along? I know I have.

Once you become retired this can easily happen to you, because some people will assume that you either have nothing better to do, or that you might be bored.

What activities do you want to do most of all when you retire? Do you want to spend time with family (mostly grandkids), golf, fish, read, or do puzzles? No matter what it is, everyone has a different agenda of what they want to do when they retire. I have a client who retired and thought he needed to play golf; all of his friends were playing golf and kept asking him to come play a round. He bought all of the golf equipment and started taking lessons. After a couple of years, he just wasn't having fun. He said that he liked being outdoors, and liked the exercise, but golf was just too frustrating for him.

Has this ever happened to you? Because of your situation in life, do people think you should be doing something, whether it is golf, the symphony, or playing bridge?

Don't think this list needs to be major things. They can be reading, jigsaw puzzles, golf . . . anything that you really want to do once you retire. They could be anything that you wish you could spend more time doing now.

I have clients who golf almost every day. I know that if I call them before four o'clock in the afternoon they will not be home, unless the weather is too bad to play golf. One morning I called when it was thirty-eight degrees outside; my client wasn't home so I left a message. He called me back at about 4:00 p.m. and he had been out playing golf. He said it wasn't windy, and the sun was out so it wasn't bad. This might be true, but it was still only thirty-eight degrees.

I have other clients who fish every day; they are the same way. In weather not fit for man nor beast, they are still out there fishing on some lake or river.

As crazy as this might sound, unless an offer comes up that they really have an interest in, they always have something better to do. I am not suggesting that you become fanatical about something just so you have an excuse to get out of doing things that you would rather not do. I am merely pointing out that, if you want to do something once you retire, make it a priority.

Since 1990, I have been working with people who have worked and planned for retirement. I have seen hundreds of people go from work to retirement. One of the most common things people say to me after they retire is, "I don't know how I had time to work before; I am so busy now."

It is usually a good thing to be active once you have retired, and do all of the things that you wanted to do while you were working. Once retired, some people have so much fun that they are often busy traveling and doing the things they most enjoy. Other retirees wish they had more time to slow down and relax. No matter if you are the type that likes to be on the go all of the time, or if you like to relax and take it easy, you should be able to do what you want. You didn't spend all of those years having someone tell you what to do just so you could retire and have someone else tell you what to do. With a little bit of planning, you should be able to do just what you want to do.

When you retire, some people will assume that you have nothing better to do and are probably bored. They will volunteer you for everything that comes along in which they have an interest. You might have to learn how to say "no" if you find yourself getting involved in things you would really rather not get involved with. Saying "no" is much easier to do if you have a prior commitment, because you can say, " I am sorry, I already have plans."

Saying no, if you do not already have plans, requires a little more discipline. We all want to help, and we don't like to say no to people we like. So, it can be very difficult to turn someone down when they ask us to help. Volunteering for a worthy cause can be one of the most rewarding things we can do. But, when we get over-committed, we tend to not get the benefit or perform as well as we should. For a lot of retirees it will not be boredom that they will have to combat once they have stopped going to work everyday. Instead, it will be over-commitment.

People who assume you have excess of time on your hands might try to keep you occupied. They might think that you will want to do something to stay occupied, because they think you are sitting around the house feeling bored. Some of the activities people will ask you to do will be things that you have an interest in, and will be things that you would be happy to do. Others might be something that you have no interest in, or don't want to do.

If you have priorities, it is easy to say, "I'm sorry, I already have something else planned." And, if you tell the people how active you are and how busy you have become, they will be less likely to try to volunteer you for everything that comes along.

A client of mine was retiring, and she had grandchildren that lived close to her. In preparing for her retirement, we discussed what she was going to do with her spare time. She said, "I am not retiring so I can be a built-in nanny for my grandkids."

Now, don't take this statement the wrong way; she loves her

grandkids as much as any grandparent ever could. She just didn't want her children to think that, because she was retired and lived close, they could use her as their sole babysitting resource anytime they wanted. Does she babysit her grandkids? You bet she does, several times a week, and she loves it. What she did was establish some ground rules with her children so they would know what to expect from her. Now her children know that if they want her to watch the grandchildren, they need to plan in advance.

I have another client in a very similar situation. I spoke with her when she was not happy with her daughter. Her daughter was divorced and had two young children. On a Thursday evening, the daughter called to say that she needed her to watch the children from Friday through Tuesday. The reason was that the daughter's new boyfriend was taking her to Vegas the next day for a long weekend. The mother was very upset with her daughter. She told me she was opposed to the situation for several different reasons. She didn't want to disappoint the daughter, so she agreed to do something she didn't want to do. She had never set a guideline for her daughter regarding babysitting services. She had simply made an open-ended offer, the kind that we all have made at one time or another in our lives. When her daughter was going through the divorce she said, "Anything I can do to help you with the children, just let me know."

This was a long, exhausting four days for her, and she resented her daughter for leaving her kids with her on such short notice.

Situations like these are why it is so important to manage expectations before you retire. Lay down the ground rules so your family and friends will know what they can or should expect from you. We all want to help our children; we just don't want to be taken advantage of.

By setting expectations in advance, you have two positive effects on the parent/child relationship. First, it reduces hard feelings and resentment that can build if expectations are not the same. Second, it helps others realize that your time is important.

Are you saying to yourself, "My children and I have an understanding about this sort of thing." Are you certain they have the same understanding of it that they do? Are they aware of this understanding? An understanding isn't necessarily an agreement. It is well worth the time to have a conversation with family and friends about what things you are available to help out with. Of course, in an emergency, you would want to be available. But, you would like to avoid the call at four thirty in the afternoon of their anniversary, the one asking if you can watch the kids that night so they can go out. Those calls can create discontent and resentment on one of the persons involved, if not all.

My wife and I do this to my mother-in-law from time to time. My wife assures me that her mother loves to watch our children, therefore it is okay. If she doesn't want to watch our children, but didn't have the heart to tell us, she will not be happy watching our children.

The reason I talk about family so much in this chapter, is because you cannot change your family members. I have heard more complaints about family, in regard to a lack of respect involving the time topic, than all others combined. You can disown your children, and you can move and not leave a forwarding address. You cannot talk to them for thirty years, but they are still your children. When you are old and need companionship or assistance, it is most likely going to come from your family Therefore, it is in your best interest to maintain a good relationship with them.

Friends, on the other hand, tend to be less likely than your children to monopolize your time. But, they still can if you let them.

Don't misunderstand me regarding this topic; I am not suggesting that once you retire you should devote all of your time and effort to yourself, becoming a Scrooge with your time. What I am suggesting is you manage your time to help your family and friends in a way that is good for all parties involved. This is because if you lend assistance to someone when you really don't want to, you might become resentful toward that person for having to spend your time doing whatever it is that you didn't want to do. This means that you most likely won't get the great feeling you normally get for helping someone out, and you may not perform as well as you could.

Most of us have had this happen to us at one time or another in our lives. We feel great about helping someone out because it was the right thing to do. We do a great job and feel really good about ourselves for helping out. We have also had to help someone because we felt obligated to him or her. We felt horrible, because the whole time we were thinking about how we were wasting our time and they were thinking, "Why did they even bother showing up?"

Once retired, if you stop helping others and only focus on yourself, you can fall into depression and a downward spiral. We feel better about ourselves and tend to be happier when we help others.

When God designed us, he did something amazing. He made it so our brains would kick out a little shot of pleasure, called an endorphin, any time we do something good. These endorphins create a sense of well being and happiness. It is almost like giving a rat some cheese at the end of the maze. Do something good, here is a shot of endorphins. Finish a task, here is another shot. Exercise or laugh, still more endorphins. Smiling, taking a walk, and even some foods will release endorphins.

Endorphins are not a free pass. If you do something good for someone, and resent the fact that you are doing it, no endorphins. I don't know this for a fact, but I believe that there is a chemical that works just the opposite of endorphins. If you do something bad, you get a shot of something that makes you feel bad.

I have seen this happen more than once when people retire. They used to rely on their jobs for their sense of accomplishment, and once they retire that sense is gone. If they do not have anything to replace it with, they sink into a depressed state. They will often languish there until they find something that they feel is worthwhile. In many studies I have read, depression appears to play a major factor in shortening your life.

Enough of the depressing stuff; lets get back to the topic of friends. I read an account of a conversation between two ladies in an article about time management. The conversation went something like this.

Lady 1: "I heard that you volunteered to handle the planning for the big annual event this year."

Lady 2: "I don't know if you can call it volunteering, So and so called me and asked if I could do it, and when I hesitated she made me feel guilty about it."

Lady 1: "Yes, she called me as well, but I was already committed for something else."

Even though I have seen this type of thing happen frequently, I didn't use personal experience because someone might read this book and think it was a situation involving them.

This conversation is probably not that uncommon in many of our lives. We all are asked to do things from time to time that we don't want to do. We have no other reason to say no to them other than that we just don't want to. If it is a worthy cause we tend to go ahead and do it, regardless of how we feel.

It is important to have priorities and expectations set before you retire. This way, when you do the task that you have been asked to do, people will be grateful for the great job you did and you might even feel good about it once you have finished. But, if you are doing the job that you don't want to do, while you are working along you might not be happy thinking about all of the other things you would rather be doing.

Do you tend to do a better job when you are happy to be doing it, or when you are dreading and resenting every minute of it.

So, let's go back to the example of the two ladies having a conversation. The lady who had volunteered for this big task was not looking forward to doing it. She is most likely not going to put her heart into the project. She probably resents the woman who roped her into the project. Since she doesn't really want to do it, she will probably not do the best job that she could. Then, some of the people at that organization will start to think of her as not fit to handle important tasks. She will not get all of the "job well done" comments that she would have gotten if she had her heart into the project.

I have said it before and I will say it again; it is important to manage the expectations others have of your time.

How can you manage other's expectations if you have no expectations of your own? When you are preparing for retirement, set your priorities so you can start planning for the things that are most important to you.

CHAPTER 9

Staying Healthy, Mentally and Physically

"A person too busy to take care of his health is like a mechanic too busy to take care of his tools." —Spanish Proverb

I have two clients who recently retired. They were both about sixty-one years old, very active with travel, writing, and family. Neither of them appeared to have any trouble getting around, and they looked as though they would have a great retirement ahead of them in the financial, physical, and mental sense. They said something that surprised me; they told me that they needed to start an exercise routine to get in shape. Since they were both very active and looked to be in pretty good shape, I asked them why they needed to get in better shape. They told me that they wanted to start some type of exercise program now, so they could remain mobile and active when they are in their eighties.

Most of us don't think that far in advance. We think about money and health, but we don't tend to think about being able to get around when we are eighty plus years old.

Between now and your final days on earth you will probably want to be able to do as many things as you possibly can. You can easily have ten to thirty years ahead of you, if not more, to do what you want to do. You don't want to spend this time being pushed around in a wheelchair if you can help it. You want to be able to go, do, and see whatever you can whenever you can. Your best chance of being able to do the things you want to do, for as long as you possibly can, is a little preparation. This little preparation is an exercise program to help you remain flexible and physically able, so you can extend the time you have to do the things you want to do.

Numerous studies have shown that physical activity that leads to increased strength and flexibility in your fifties and sixties will dramatically improve your chances of being more mobile when you are in your seventies, eighties, and beyond.

Retirement isn't just about not having to go to work everyday; it is about the freedom to get out there and do what you want to do. After you have gotten to this point, when you can retire after so many years of work, don't you want to be able to enjoy your retirement for as long as you possibly can?

We have all seen this happen before; someone retires and almost immediately goes into a sharp decline mentally, physically, or both. This is not an uncommon event for many retirees. Many experts link this to a lack of physical and mental stimulation, and a general lack of activity. Some studies link this sort of decline to a lack of accomplishment, the sense of well-being that occurs when you achieve something significant. Others have associated this type of decline to an increased stress level dealing with finances or fear of death.

No matter what the cause, we don't want it to happen to you. There have been numerous studies done regarding staying healthy and active in retirement. We will review several of the ways that people I know have stayed healthy and happy well into their nineties and beyond.

My grandmother was an active woman. She walked everyday, wrote in her journal, quilted, and did so many other things. She was amazingly sharp for a woman of ninety-four. She also had to take insulin for her diabetes for over fifty years.

Long before she retired from teaching, my grandmother started walking around the halls of Lindbergh Elementary School where she taught second grade. Every morning, before classes would start, she walked for a certain period of time through the halls. Not only did it provide her with exercise, but it also gave her some quiet time to think and prepare for her day. The morning routine kept her body active and her mind sharp.

My grandmother was also slightly stubborn . . . hardheaded some might have said. When she retired she continued this routine, only now it wasn't through the halls of a school, it was through her neighborhood. If the weather was bad, she exercised in the house.

She attributed her many years of good health and mobility after she retired to this activity. She would talk about teachers who had retired about the same time she did who weren't active. They weren't as happy or healthy as she was, and Grandmother knew why.

After several years of this exercise routine, she got a dog. It was not just any dog but a slightly hyper cocker spaniel named Honey. She would take her dog for a walk everyday regardless of rain or shine, sleet or snow, or even ice. You might be wondering why an older lady would take a dog for a walk when it is icy. I don't know; it must be a dog thing. Unless you have a dog you probably wouldn't understand (and I did mention she was stubborn). This happened not once, but twice. She took her dog for a walk when it was icy outside, and the dog caused her to fall. The first time, the dog took off chasing a cat or some small animal; I don't know what caused the second fall. The first time she broke her pelvis, and the second time she broke her leg. Falls are one of the most common accidents to happen to us as we get older. They also are among the most debilitating things that can happen to our bodies.

As we get older, our bodies don't heal as fast as they once did.

After these two incidents, she needed a walker to get around. Although this was a bit of a setback for her, it did not seem to slow her down much. She was still very active and living alone.

Staying active, and regular exercise, can help you have a longer, happier, healthier, and a more mobile retirement. Try not to expose yourself to risky situations to help you to avoid some unnecessary injuries. We are not as young as we used to be, and some injuries can force us to change our way of life. Just because you lose some mobility doesn't mean you have to give up your active lifestyle.

I told you this story about the loss of mobility for a simple reason; I have seen far too many people lose some mobility and simply give up on life. They sit in a chair and watch life and the world pass them by. It is sad to see, and it doesn't have to happen to you.

I have read several studies linking mental and physical inactivity to increased deterioration of people's mental and physical health. Our mental and physical health are often linked. A healthy body usually equals a healthy mind, and vice versa.

This doesn't mean you need to train for a marathon or climb to the top of Mount Everest; it simply means that it is very beneficial for you to stay active. It is very easy and enjoyable to take a walk, work out at the gym, or play any type of sport (rugby or football might not be the best sports to play if you want to keep your mobility). I have played basketball with people who are in their seventies that could really run up and down the court.

You might be thinking to yourself that you have known people who were active whose minds deteriorated, or who are confined to a wheelchair now. Unfortunately, just like life and the stock market, there are no guarantees when it comes to mental or physical health. You can do everything possible to stay healthy and still have bad things happen to you, just like you can do everything bad and pass on at 102, never being sick a day in your life. What you are doing by staying active is increasing the chances that you will stay mentally sharp and physically mobile along with enjoying life.

A client of mine smoked heavily for fifty years, before she quit at age seventy-five; She is now ninety-five. Just because you smoke doesn't mean you will get lung cancer. By smoking, you are increasing your chances of getting lung cancer, but it does not guarantee that you will get it. On the same token, not smoking doesn't guarantee you won't get it.

We try to minimize our risks to help us avoid winding up in a bad situation. The more risk we take, the greater the chance that something bad will happen to us.

Falls are a major cause for older people to lose their mobility prematurely. There are two types of falls. The first type is that you step onto something slick, and you slip and fall. The second is when you lose your balance trying to reach something. Both can be very painful and can be downright deadly.

A regular exercise program that involves strength training can help reduce your chances of losing your balance and falling over. This doesn't mean you have to start lifting weights and pumping iron on a regular basis. Exercise programs like Pilates, yoga, and aerobics accomplish very similar things. Most communities will have an exercise program set up for retirees either through the "Y" or other community organizations. If you live in an area that doesn't offer this type of program, you can buy a video to work out with at home.

This morning I did a Pilates video, and I have to confess my workout routine has not been that routine here of late. This video helps my flexibility and gives me the exercise I need to get the day started off right. My knees, elbows, and back really bother me when I don't do some type of workout like this. Not only can strength training help reduce your chance of a fall. It can also increase bone density, which may reduce the effects of osteoporosis.

Now that we have discussed how to reduce the risk of losing-your-balance type falls, let's discuss the falls that occur when we climb up on something.

I had a ninety-five-year-old client who fell off of a ladder pulling ivy vines off of the side of her building. This fall took her out of her home and placed her in an assisted living facility for the next nine years. That's right, she lived to be 104. After she recovered from the fall, she remained very active, and could have returned to her own home and lived on her own. At this point in time, she didn't want to move again and she liked her assisted care facility.

Throughout her life she was very independent, and even though there were many people that lived in her building that were willing to help pull the vines down, she insisted on doing it herself. Was she wrong for climbing up a ladder at her age? In hindsight it probably wasn't the best decision she ever made, but would she have been this active if she didn't do things like that? Probably not.

Her response, when people questioned her decision to climb the ladder was, "There was nothing wrong with me climbing the ladder, but I should not have fallen off."

The older we get, the slower our reaction time becomes. When our reaction time slows, we cannot use our balance and movement to prevent falls as effectively as we used to. We need to avoid slick surfaces, standing on things, and reaching off to the sides in order to reach something. We do this in order to reduce the risks of a fall if we can.

Along with exercise, a proper diet can help you increase your chances of a long, active, and happy retirement. Eating too much or eating unhealthy foods can increase your weight. Increased weight puts more stress on your knees, hips, and back. These joints need to last as long as possible, so the less stress we can put on them the better off you will be.

One common mistake is thinking that drinking diet soda isn't bad for you. If you drink nothing but diet soda it is true that you are not consuming a lot of calories, but you might be consuming a lot of sodium, caffeine, and chemicals that could have a negative impact on your body. Besides the stuff you are consuming, what are you not consuming? You are not consuming calcium, vitamins, or minerals for the most part, because soda replaces the other beverages that you would drink.

Many studies have shown that people who eat a lot of junk food and drink a lot of sodas have higher rates of depression. Retirement should be the time of your life, not the time to suffer with depression.

Many fast foods and junk foods are highly processed. They no longer have the fiber, whole grains, or vitamins that freshly prepared foods have. It is very important for our bodies to have foods that are rich in nutrients and fiber. Staying away from highly processed foods can help your body and your mind stay healthy.

Do you remember the "Twinkie Defense?" It happened in San Francisco in the late 1970s. A person went off the deep end and shot a couple of people in city hall. His attorneys tried to say that it was his excessive junk food diet that led to the rampage. Even though he was still found guilty, the defense did lead to several studies of diet on mental health; the findings are fairly conclusive that a good diet can increase your brain function.

In a very recent study, there appears to be a link between the consumption of raw fruits and vegetables, and a reduction in Alzheimer's disease.

We want to eat healthy and exercise to increase our chances of a long, healthy life; the healthier we are the happier we tend to be.

I always think it is so funny to call a client and ask, "Are you in the middle of anything, or is this a good time to talk?" They respond that they are working on some sort of puzzle or mental challenge game. I have never had a client who worked at puzzles or mind games lose their mental facilities at an early age. I believe that anything that challenges the mind reduces your chance for mental deterioration. It is like a brisk walk for your brain. So, anytime you read, play a musical instrument, or work on puzzles your brain gets the activity it needs to stay in shape.

The main thing you want to avoid is sitting on the couch and watching TV all day long. Not only is it bad for the body, but for the mind as well. Stay active and use your body and your mind on a regular basis; you will be glad you did.

We are very fortunate to be growing older at this time in history. Not that long ago there were not many activities for people to do once they retired. Now, there are numerous trips that cater to people over age sixty-five; there are continuing education classes offered at many colleges and universities. And, there my personal favorite . . . the elder hostel.

An elder hostel is a short study, usually four to seven days, where you travel to a location, stay in a dorm or other accommodation, and gain knowledge on a particular topic of interest.

I have clients who just got back from a hiking trip in Texas. My grandmother did an origami (oriental paper-folding) class in Michigan. Elder hostels are available around the world and offer many different topics. A good resource for elder hostels worldwide is www.elderhostel.org. You can go to this web site and choose a course that you would like to take, and find a location that interests you. There are also numerous books and publications at your public library about elder hostels, their locations, and the courses they offer.

Elder hostels are a great way to learn new things and meet new people. With such a variety of subjects and locations, there is most likely an elder hostel that would interest you somewhere.

Another way to explore new places and learn new things is travel geared for retirees. I have seen brochures for these types of trips ranging from local bus trips that last a day, to an around-the-world trip using multiple means of transportation. These trips usually include guides to explain different things along the way.

A bank or travel agency usually sponsors these trips. If your bank doesn't offer such trips, go to your travel agent and see if they have any offerings that interest you.

The thing I like most about these trips is that everything is taken care of for you; you don't need to do much planning. Some people do not like the structured trips, where what you will do when is planned in advance. But, it is a pleasant, almost worry-free way to travel and learn about different things.

It doesn't matter what activities you choose to do once you are retired; it matters that you choose to do something. Do the things that you love and enjoy. Use your retirement years to go, see, and do what you have always wanted to do.

Retirement shouldn't be the end of your journey; it should be the beginning of a grand odyssey. Make the most of it.

CHAPTER 10
Retirement Planning in a Nutshell

Decide what you want to do once you retire.

If you don't have a hobby or interests, get at least one.

Make sure you have the financial resources in order to retire the way you want to. (Increase savings and pay down debt)

Decide when to retire.

Get your life organized and make sure the loose ends are tied up before you retire.

Prepare for the unexpected so you don't have to return to work in a few years.

Start exercising and eating right.

A little planning and preparation can make the difference between a great retirement experience, where you are able to do what you have always dreamed of, or a stressful time where you are wondering how you are going to make ends meet. I would much rather spend my retirement years living my dreams, wouldn't you?

I hope you have enjoyed this part of the book, and find it helpful with planning your retirement.

I have included a reference section to answer questions you might have about Medicare, Social Security, investments, and investments strategies, along with a glossary of commonly used financial terms that you might like a definition for.

CHAPTER 11
Reference Section

I. Social Security:

A big question is usually, "When should I start to take my Social Security?"

The quick answer is: At age sixty-two, you can start to draw Social Security at a reduced level. Full Social Security retirement age as of 2009 is 66. This reduced benefit is approximately 75 percent of its payout if you start your benefits at age sixty-two versus waiting until you are 66. This amount moves up each year until age sixty-six if you put off taking distributions. If you are a married couple with a nonworking spouse, or a spouse who has earned dramatically less income than the main breadwinner, the nonworking spouse can draw half of the working spouse's Social Security benefit.

For example, let's say you have a Social Security benefit of $1,000 per month. If your spouse is eligible, they will receive $500 per month, even if they never contributed to the Social Security system.

The big question usually is, "Should I start my benefits at age sixty-two or wait until age sixty-six?" That is a good question, but unfortunately there is no "one size fits all" rule when it comes to Social Security benefits. For example, if you start your benefits at age sixty-two versus sixty-six, you are receiving 75 percent of what your benefit would have been if you had worked until you were sixty-six. If your full benefit would have been $20,000 per year, you now will receive $15,000 per year. You can figure approximately twelve years until you break even. In other words, if you wait to draw income until age sixty-six, you will have drawn out about the same amount of money at age seventy-four as you would have if you started your distributions at age sixty-two. These are approximate numbers and do not take into account the cost of living adjustments.

In theory, if you live beyond age seventy-four, you would have been better off waiting to receive your benefits at age sixty-six. If you pass on prior to seventy-four, you would have been better off taking it early. Statistics indicate that if you are sixty-two years old, you will most likely make it beyond the age of seventy-four, according to the U.S. Department of Health and Human Services 2004 life expectancy table. This being said, many experts feel it is better to wait until you reach your full Social Security age before starting your benefits.

Another consideration is the earnings cap placed on your benefit prior to age sixty-five. This earnings cap limits your Social Security benefit if you earn over a specified amount of money in income from other sources. Once you reach sixty-five, this cap goes away.

Before you spend endless hours trying to figure out what your Social Security benefits will be, make an appointment with your local Social Security office to get the full details of your benefits. Trying to figure this out on your own, or over the phone, is a long, drawn- out, and unnecessary process. I have found the people staffing the Social Security offices to be knowledgeable. They are very helpful in answering questions and instructing you regarding the many options you have when it comes to your benefits. If you would like to do your own research on the Internet, Social Security's website is http://www.ssa.gov. You can also call to set up and appointment at 800-772-1213. Be warned, sometimes there is a lengthy hold time on this number. You can find the local office either from the website or your phone book. The problem I have encountered by dropping in without an appointment is that sometimes they are short-staffed or booked with appointments, and you might not be able to meet with someone that day. No matter how you set up your appointment, I would highly recommend you meet with one of their representatives prior to filling out your claim form.

Many of you may wonder if Social Security will still be around when you retire. The answer is yes, in some form or another. If you plan on drawing Social Security soon, chances are that you will not see many changes in eligibility, benefit amount, or cost of living adjustment. But, if you have twenty or more years before you are eligible to receive retirement benefits, you will probably not have the same benefit package that current Social Security recipients have. The reason being is simple. When Social Security was first introduced in 1935, it was to be a social safety net for the unemployed, survivors of workers, and the people who couldn't afford to retire. Since the time of it being implemented, benefits have been increased, politicians have used its funds to fund other programs, and many new features and enhancements have been added.

Love it or hate it, the Social Security system is the largest government program in the world. The White House budget projection for 2008 had Social Security making up 20.9 percent of the total US budget. Medicare is in second place with 20.4 percent of the total United States government's budget.

You might wonder why this would have an impact on you or your situation. Very simply, the seventy million baby boomers that are starting to receive Social Security are living longer, and older Americans as a demographic are the fastest growing segment of the US population. So, we have more people receiving Social Security benefits than ever before; that number is going up daily.

What concerns many people is not the number of recipients, but the ratio of people paying into the Social Security system versus the number of people receiving benefits. When Ida May Fuller was issued the first Social Security check on January 31, 1940, the average U.S. life expectancy was about sixty-four years. This is how they did the math. If you give people benefits when they are sixty-five, and the average life expectancy is sixty-four, then the average contributor to the Social Security system would draw very few benefits. Now that the average life expectancy is over seventy-five years of age, combined with the fact that now you can start receiving benefits as early as age sixty-two, the average recipient will receive many more payments than they used to.

By the way, Ida May Fuller drew Social Security benefits until her death in 1975. She received benefits for over thirty-five years, which was almost unthinkable in the 1940s. Now, it is fairly common.

According to the Social Security Administration, when Ida May received her first check there were about 150 workers paying into the system for each recipient. By the time she received her last check, the ratio had dropped to 3.2 workers paying in for every person receiving a check. The ratio is now 3.3 workers for each recipient, according to the Social Security Administration. That ratio has held steady since the mid-seventies, but is expected to drop to 2.3 workers for every recipient by the year 2025, as people have fewer children and retirees are living longer.

This becomes a major issue because the fewer workers you have paying into the system, the more they have to pay to support the system, or the fewer the benefits can be paid out. When Social Security was first introduced, the tax rate was 2 percent. One percent was paid by the employer, and 1 percent was paid by the employee. Now it is 12.4 percent, with the employee and employer each contributing 6.2 percent.

According to the 2005 report from the Social Security trustees, the current system will be able to meet its current obligation until 2041 (if their projections are correct). Don't think because of these numbers that your benefits will remain the same until 2041 and then disappear. Congress will likely be forced to take some type of corrective action to keep the Social Security system solvent prior to the time that it runs out of money.

Social Security has been on the brink of bankruptcy before, and changes were made to keep it solvent. I cannot imagine Congress allowing the Social Security system to go out of business.

II. Medicare:

The major question regarding Medicare is, "Am I eligible to receive benefits?" The answer is "maybe."

If you are eligible for Social Security benefits either on your own or through your spouse, you should be eligible to receive Medicare. Medicare is the second largest program of the US government, just slightly behind Social Security as a percentage of the total federal budget, and is growing rapidly. As Americans age, more people are becoming eligible for the program and new medical procedures are being introduced to prolong our lives.

Medicare has four different plans, A, B, C, and D.

Medicare Part A eligibility occurs when you turn sixty-five. Unlike Social Security, there is no early eligibility or reduced benefit for early enrollment.

If you are eligible for Social Security or a railroad pension, you should be able to receive Medicare Part A coverage. You may be eligible for Medicare prior to age sixty-five if you are disabled or are in the end-stage renal disease.

Enrollment is easy; if you start to draw Social Security prior to age sixty-five you are automatically enrolled in Part A and B. If you are not receiving Social Security benefits prior to age sixty-five, you should enroll for Medicare three months prior to turning sixty-five. You can do this by calling the Social Security Administration to enroll at 800-772-1213.

Coverage is fairly straightforward:

Part A covers your major medical, for example: surgery and hospital stays.

Part B covers medical exams and outpatient procedures.

Part C combines A and B in something called Medicare Advantage, which is not available in all areas.

Part D is the prescription plan benefit.

If you are eligible for Medicare Part A coverage, there is no cost. There is a cost associated with Parts B, C, and D. If you are not eligible for Medicare coverage, you can buy into any of the parts of this program.

There are too many scenarios and possibilities to discuss in detail in this book, so I am just going to cover the most basic information. Before you drop your private insurance because you are eligible for Medicare, you should contact Medicare to have your specific questions answered. Make sure that any procedures or medications you are currently on are covered by Medicare before dropping your private insurance.

The rate of growth of the Medicare system is causing alarm to many people who follow it closely. As its budget continues to grow, many are wondering how we will pay for this program going forward. This becomes an issue to you because of the high cost of health care in your later years.

A friend of mine just became eligible for Medicare; the last year he paid for private health insurance cost him around $18,000 for coverage for both he and his wife. This is a very large sum of money to most of us, and it would be unaffordable to most. He had a very good policy that had features that most of us wouldn't have paid for, and he had some medical issues. If he had done away with some of the features, he could have dropped that premium down to the $8,000 to $10,000 range for the type of coverage he wanted. There are some types of health insurance that are more affordable than that.

Health insurance is a major issue for most people who consider early retirement. You either need to be covered by an employer plan or be prepared to pay a large amount for private insurance coverage.

In 2008, the Medicare eligibility standard was age sixty-five. There are some discussions of increasing that age to sixty-seven or seventy, with the possibility of being able to buy in at an earlier age.

If this increased age were to occur, many people planning on retiring at age sixty-five might need to consider retiring at a later date, or spending more money out of pocket than they had previously planned.

When you meet with the Social Security Administration, they should be able to answer many of your questions about Medicare as well. If not, they can provide you with the information of who you will need to speak with.

III. Investment Risk and Returns

If it sounds too good to be true, it probably is.

We don't have time or space in this book to be a "how-to" on investing with an in-depth view on the topic; there are hundreds of books about how to invest. I just wanted to cover the basics of some of the more common mistakes I have seen people make, and some basic principals to follow when investing.

I met with a client who was planning on retiring within a year. To help me evaluate how much income she could receive from her account I ran a Monte Carlo simulation. A Monte Carlo simulation is a system that shows what the chances are that you will run out of money given your time frame, asset allocation, and the distributions you are taking from the account. I input all of her information so she could see how much income she could expect from her current allocation. After finishing the analysis, I told her that, with her age and current investments, she could receive about 6 percent from her account. With her age of 65 and assuming twenty-five years of distribution she had a good chance of not running out of money in her lifetime. She was very disappointed with the distribution rate I had come up with. She had a friend who had told her that she could easily withdraw 10 percent of her account value annually to live on.

Just a refresher on this: According to the Sungard Analytics, if you were to withdraw 10 percent per year from your account, it shows about a 10 percent chance you could run out of money in Ten years. It shows a nearly 50 percent chance of your running out of money in twenty years, and over a 60 percent chance of running out of money in thirty years. I have seen many charts and studies that show a much greater chance of running out of money with a 10 percent distribution rate.

The reason the Sungard model shows a better chance for success is because there are no expenses to run the portfolio; it uses indexes to model the portfolio. It also assumes index level performance, which less than 20 percent of the mutual funds accomplish on an annual basis. In other words, you would have to do incredibly well, and keep your costs incredibly low, to match the numbers that Sungard is using. It also assumes an annual rebalancing of the portfolio. Rebalancing the portfolio each year may help prolong the life of your account by not getting over-weighted in any single asset category.

Most of us would feel comfortable if we had a 90 percent chance of our investments still being around when we pass on. So, if you don't plan on being around in ten years, this is probably a good amount for you to withdraw on an annual basis.

I personally do not like the fifty/fifty probability of running out of money in twenty years. After all, the average retiree will spend more than twenty years in retirement.

If you go to the Internet and Google the phrase "running out of money table" you will find many illustrations showing similar percentages.

Can you pull out 10 percent of your portfolio each year for a lifetime and not run out of money? Sure, there is that possibility. Your portfolio might be able to provide this level of income for you but the odds are against you. Why take that chance?

The later in life you retire, the higher percentage of your total assets you should be able to withdraw. The more conservatively you invest, the less you should withdraw.

I have a client who thinks the U.S. financial system is a house of cards, ready to fall in at any time. Therefore, he wanted nothing but government bonds, and nothing with a maturity over five years. When he retired, we could buy five-year Treasury bonds yielding close to 6 percent. According to www.bloomberg.com, the yield on the same five-year Treasury bonds, as of September 23, 2008, was less than 3 percent. So, if you want to invest in short-term Treasury bonds, you will need to keep your withdrawals under 4 percent to have a good chance that you will not outlive your money.

Investment Products:

Many salespeople claim the way around the risk of running out of money is with specific insurance products. I am not an advocate for or an opponent of most of these products; I just want you to understand what they are and how they work.

Most people do not understand what an annuity is, because they have only seen the fixed annuities or an immediate annuity.

A fixed annuity has a fixed term and a fixed percentage interest rate. An insurance company guarantees your funds, based on the financial strength, and claims paying ability of the issuing insurance company; the interest you earn is tax deferred. Tax deferred means you only pay taxes on that money when you pull it out of the annuity. Even fixed annuities have become more complex; many of them pay a high interest rate in the beginning and then lower the interest rate a few years into the contract. They also may be subject to a market value adjustment if you withdraw funds or surrender them before they mature.

A market value adjustment is an adjustment made to the value of your distribution. It reflects the difference in performance between the annuity and the underlying investments that the insurance company has invested in to fund your annuity.

An immediate annuity is where you give the insurance company a lump sum of money, and they pay out a stream of income for a stated period of time (usually a certain period or life). Once you annuitize, in exchange for the guaranteed income, access to principal may be limited or not allowed at all. And, while your income payment will not fluctuate due to market volatility, your income stream does not grow to offset inflation.

Many people do this because it guarantees them a certain level of income each month. This amount may be higher than what they could get elsewhere, because they are receiving some of their principal along with interest in each check.

There are also two very different types of annuities that have been developed. These are the variable annuity and the equity-index annuity.

The contract owner has the ability to invest in assets in various sub-accounts. These are called separate accounts because these assets are held separately from the insurance company's fixed accounts. If you invest in a variable annuity, your performance is based on the returns on the separate account, minus expenses. Therefore, your returns are variable on the performance of these separate accounts. If you buy a variable annuity, you will select from a number of investment options in order to form your asset allocation. Most variable annuities have several separate accounts to choose from, covering many different asset categories. Many insurance companies now offer asset allocations funding options to make the investment process easier for the investor. You simply check a box that corresponds with your risk tolerance, time horizon, and investment objectives.

Variable annuities have some guarantees associated with them that other types of investments do not. They also tend to have more costs associated with them.

The cost of a variable annuity is usually an internal cost that you will never see, because it is taken from the performance of your investments. Stated costs of variable annuities, including the insurance cost, fund expenses, administrative expense, and mortality expense, tend to run from around 1 percent on the low end to about 4 percent on the high end. So, if you have invested in an annuity with a 4 percent expense ratio, and your underlying investment has produced 10 percent, you will see a net return of 6 percent. A mistake many investors make in variable annuities is being too conservative. If you have an annuity with an average stated expense of 2.2 percent, and invest in nothing but bond funds that average 5 percent, you will net only 2.8 percent. I have actually seen instances where people invested in short-term bond funds inside an annuity, and their investment returns were less than their annuity expenses. They were actually losing money on a very safe investment.

Another type of annuity is the equity-index annuity. These are products that, in most cases, have a guaranteed minimum interest rate. The also have the possibility of a higher interest rate if the investment it is linked to should perform better than the minimum interest rate. This sounds great; you can have a guarantee, and if the market goes up, you get to participate in the increase.

The problem with many of these annuities is that they are complicated and, in my opinion, often not quite as good a deal as they appear to be. It sounds so simple; a guaranteed rate of return if the market doesn't perform well, and a higher rate of return if the market does perform well. What is so confusing about that?

Many of these products have performance caps and participation rates. These are limits on your upside potential. If your equity-indexed annuity should have a cap rate of 8 percent and the market does 20 percent, you get 8 percent. You are capped at 8 percent, and no matter how the market performs, you cannot do better than that. A participation rate is the percentage of the upside you get to participate in. So, you have a 75 percent participation rate and the market goes up 10 percent; you make 7.5 percent. This is true unless the cap rate is lower than the participation rate; in that case, you get whichever number is lower.

Are you confused yet? If not, it gets even better. When the market drops you can still lose value; it just won't go below the guaranteed rate of return, unless you want to pull it out before the surrender charge has ended. Then, you may be subject to a hefty surrender charge and a market value adjustment.

The surrender charge is easy to explain: You buy a product and it has no upfront sales charge. You see no decrease in account value when your money goes in because it has a contingent-deferred sales charge. The sales charge is contingent on you holding the product until maturity; at maturity, you can surrender your contract without seeing a sales charge. But, if you should surrender this annuity before maturity, you may be subject to a surrender charge on the amount.

Let's say you bought a twenty-year contract. You have held this contract for five years and decide you need the money. Based on a ten-year surrender schedule, you might have to pay 20 percent of your account value in surrender charges. For example, if your account value is $100,000, you surrender your contract and you receive $80,000 after the surrender charge. That is the case if you do not have a market value adjustment as well as a surrender charge. If you are not confused yet, the market value adjustment should do the trick.

Some annuity contracts have a market value adjustment feature. If interest rates are different when you surrender your annuity than when you bought it, a market value adjustment may make the cash surrender value higher or lower. Since you and the insurance company share this risk, an annuity with an MVA feature may credit a higher rate than an annuity without that feature.

I have had salespeople for these annuities try to explain how the market value adjustment works on their product; they are unable to do so. The formulas these companies use to calculate market value adjustment tend to be very complex, and depend upon multiple factors to arrive at the final calculation.

You don't necessarily need to know what all of the definitions are regarding annuities, just what questions to ask. Whether you are buying a fixed annuity, variable annuity, or equity-indexed annuity, here are some questions that can help you better understand what you are buying::

What is the market value adjustment?

What is the maximum surrender charge?

What is the guaranteed account value at maturity?

When can I take the money out without penalty?

How much goes to my heirs when I die, and when does it get distributed to them?

What is the minimum guaranteed income I could receive?

What is the cost?

If I surrender this product in one, three, five, or ten years, what amount will I receive?

I can't tell you how many times I have had people in my office with a product that didn't work the way they thought it would. They were stuck, because the cost to get out of the product was too high.

Two cases that stand out the most in my mind involved annuities with long surrender periods.

The first case was a lady who had bought a fixed annuity with a ten-year surrender charge. She had bought this annuity from a bank and had taken a high, first-year interest rate. The second year the interest rate dropped to the minimum of 3 percent, and stayed there. This was at a time when we could buy ten-year U.S. Treasury bonds that were yielding over 5 percent, and CDs were over 6 percent. It would have cost her 12 percent of her account value to surrender the annuity and move it to a higher yielding investment. She didn't want to lose 12 percent of her money (I can't blame her) so she stayed in the annuity. When she was able to surrender her annuity without a penalty, CDs were yielding less than 3 percent. Ten-year Treasuries were yielding around 3.5 percent.

The second case was a man who, in 2003, was tired of seeing his account values drop. He received an invitation for a free dinner, where he would learn about a product that was guaranteed to hold its value if the market dropped. The product would supposedly go up in value if the market went up. He thought that this product sounded perfect for what he needed. He closed out all of his mutual funds and moved them into this equity-indexed annuity. After three years of good stock market performance, his account had barely performed above the 3 percent minimum guarantee. He bought this product because he thought that he would at least come close to performing as well as the stock market. He brought in his contract and I showed him where it had a twenty-year surrender period. If he were to surrender his policy now, he would pay over 20 percent in penalties and charges. However, those charges would have been reduced over time.

This meant that his annuity, worth $140,000, would net him a little over $105,000 if he cashed it out after three years.

Some equity-indexed annuities do not wave the surrender charges at your death. What this means is that, if you pass on before the contingent-deferred sales charge is over, your heirs cannot receive the money without paying a penalty. So, if you want to pass money onto your children when you die, make sure the surrender charge is waived at death.

Guarantees are only as good as the company making them. You could have the best guarantee in the world, but if the company making that guarantee goes out of business then the guarantee has no value.

Guarantees on your investments will have a cost; if they didn't, how could an insurance company afford to offer them? A good way to look at the guarantees offered within an annuity is to view them in the same way you view homeowner's insurance. You don't buy homeowner's insurance hoping your house will burn down; you buy it in case your house burns down. You want the insurance to cover your losses and be affordable. So, before you buy the insurance on your investments, find out what it covers and what it costs.

Understand what you are investing in before you tie your money up for five, ten or twenty years. Ask questions before you invest. How does the guarantee work? What is the minimum amount I could get out of this investment if I cash it in early? What is the rating of the company? What are its advantages and disadvantages?

Remember that there is no such thing as something for nothing. If there are guarantees they will come at a cost; you have to decide if the guarantees that a product offers is worth the price that you will have to pay.

Unfortunately, human nature is such that we tend to do the worst possible things when it comes to investing. We buy when the market is hitting all-time highs, and we sell when the market value drops. We buy short-term bonds because we don't want our money to be tied up for extended periods of time, and we have no income protection if the interest rates drop.

In the early 1980s, when interest rates hit 15 percent, how many people bought long-term bonds? The answer is, not nearly as many people as bought short-term bonds. They thought interest rates were going even higher.

When I first got into the business in 1990, the thirty-year Treasury bill was yielding about 8.65 percent. I wasn't about to invest my client's money for thirty years. I could buy a two-year bond and get 8 percent interest, and not have their money tied up for thirty years. I thought the rates would go higher. Besides, do you know what inflation would do to the value of a bond over thirty years? It could be worth half as much.

The fact of the matter, is that if you buy a thirty-year bond, or each year buy a new, one-year bond, the value is going to be the same at the end of the thirty-year period. At the time of this writing, September 2008, the thirty-year Treasury is yielding 4.35 percent. Wouldn't I have been better off buying the thirty-year bond? Of course I would have, but hindsight is twenty/twenty. If I could have known what was going to happen, I would have done just that. Unfortunately, I don't have a crystal ball. Neither does anybody else. This is why it is important to have a disciplined strategy when it comes to investing. When you let your emotions run your investment decisions, you tend to make poor decisions. There are several good bond strategies, from laddering to barbell. A laddered bond strategy simply says that you maintain a number of bonds that mature on a consistent basis, and you reinvest the maturing bonds on the next rung of the ladder.

For example, you have a $100,000 bond portfolio. You invest $10,000 into bonds maturing every year, starting in year one, and ending with year ten. At the end of the first year, a bond matures and you take the proceeds and invest it into a ten-year bond. You still have bonds that mature every year, just like when you first started the portfolio.

A barbell strategy will have most of the bonds with very short and very long maturities, and a few that are intermediate-term bonds.

Using the same figures for an example, again assume that you have a $100,000 portfolio. You take $50,000 and invest it into bonds that will mature within five years. You take the other $50,000 and invest in bonds that have maturities that are much longer . . . let's just say twenty years.

With bonds it is desirable to have liquidity, which you get from shorter-term bonds, for those times when cash is needed. It is also desirable to have income protection, which you get with some longer term bonds should interest rates drop. This would be considered trying to protect against interest rate risk.

I have seen numerous studies about the real rate-of-return of money market accounts and short-term certificates of deposit. The real rate-of-return is simply how much your investment is worth after you have paid taxes on your gain, and factored in the rate of inflation. In most cases, both money market accounts and short-term bonds don't give you much of a real rate-of-return after you factor in taxes and inflation.

For example, say you earn 5 percent on a bond, you are in the 28 percent tax bracket, and inflation runs at 3 percent that year. Since you have to pay taxes on the 5 percent you earned, your real earnings are 3.6 percent. A 5 percent interest rate times a 28 percent tax rate equals 1.4 percent amount you have to pay in taxes. A 5 percent interest rate minus 1.4 percent amount due in taxes equals 3.6 percent after-tax return. For this example let us assume that inflation is 3 percent, so you would have a real rate-of-return of .6 percent. If you want your income from your investments to keep pace with the cost of living, you will have to do better than that.

Since we are talking about bonds, let's get into municipal bonds. These bonds are issued through a state, county, city, or other similar organization. The advantage of these bonds is that they are usually tax free. I say usually, because you have to watch out, from time to time I have seen people who bought municipal bonds that they thought were tax free, and it turns out they were not. The higher your overall tax bracket, the more advantageous these types of bonds can be.

Although some people like the idea of not paying income taxes on their interest, it might not make sense for them to buy a tax-free bond with a lower yield because they are in a low tax bracket. Because of this, it is helpful to be able to calculate the tax equivalent yield. The next few paragraphs will discuss this in more detail, with examples.

Let's say you are in the 28 percent federal tax rate and 5 percent state tax rate, so your combined marginal tax rate is 33 percent. This means that for every new, taxable dollar that you earn you have to pay $.33 in taxes. To figure out if tax-free bonds are a good investment for you, you have to figure a taxable equivalent yield. Since tax-free bonds tend to pay less than their taxable counterparts, we need to be able to compare the two to see which will work out better for you.

Let's say that you are looking at two different bonds. These bonds are very similar to each other, but one is tax-free and the other is taxable. The tax-free bond has a yield of 4 percent, and the taxable bond has a yield of 5 percent. To determine which one works out better for you, we need to find the taxable equivalent yield on the tax free, or the after tax return on the taxable bond.

You start with your marginal tax rate of 33 percent. Subtract that number from 100 percent, and you get 67 percent. Sixty-seven percent is the percentage of money you get to keep after you have paid taxes on your taxable income.

To discover the taxable equivalent yield, you divide the tax-free interest rate by the percentage of money you get to keep. Four percent divided by 67 percent gives you a taxable equivalent yield of 5.97 percent. In this example, the tax-free bond gives you a higher after tax return.

You can figure your after-tax return by multiplying the percentage of money you keep after taxes by the taxable yield. In this case, you take the 67 percent and multiply that by 5 percent; you come up with 3.35 percent. So, in this example, you need to find a tax-free bond yielding over 3.35 percent tax-free yield to have a higher after tax return than the 5 percent taxable bond you were considering. Or, you need to find a taxable bond yielding over 5.97 percent taxable yield to have a higher after tax return than the 4 percent tax-free.

From time to time I do see people in very low tax brackets buying tax-free bonds. Let's take a look at someone in a 15 percent federal, and 1 percent state, marginal tax bracket. We have the same bonds; 4 percent tax-free and 5 percent taxable. Now, you take the 15 percent plus 1 percent tax rates to get a 16 percent marginal rate. One hundred percent minus 16 percent equals the return after taxes. Using the formula for taxable equivalent yield, we take the 4 percent tax-free yield and divide it by 84 percent, which gives us a 4.76 percent taxable equivalent yield. Or, we can take the 5 percent taxable yield times 84 percent to give you a 4.2 percent after tax yield.

Many states do not tax their own bonds. For example, if you live in Missouri there are no Missouri state income taxes on bonds issued in that state. But, if you live in Missouri and buy a bond from another state, you would have to pay state income taxes on that bond. Bonds from United States territories or protectorates, like Guam, Puerto Rico, and Washington, DC, are usually state-tax-free as well. You should consult a tax advisor to determine your tax rate and your state's treatment of federally tax-free income.

The alternative minimum tax, or AMT, is a tax that originally started in the early 1970s to target 155 high-income households who had so many tax deductions that they owed little or no income tax. In the thirty-eight years it has been in existence, it has affected far more than 155 households. If you earn over $100,000 a year, you will probably be subject to this tax. This is something to consider when buying a tax-free bond, since bonds that are subject to AMT tend to pay a higher interest rate than a bond not subject to AMT.

I mention this tax so you will have an idea of what "Subject to AMT" means when you are considering a bond. Due to the complex nature of the AMT tax, and the multiple eligibilities, I will not get into this tax in this book. I would defer that to your tax consultant.

The final thing I will say about investing is that human nature is to avoid pain . . . but we like gain. This can cause problems. You know investor enthusiasm is out of hand when someone utters the famous phrase, "This time it is different."

Maybe this time it is different, but I doubt it. Jeremy Siegel did a two-hundred-year study of the stock market. He found that over that time things always came back into a fairly consistent range. "But this time is different," is usually tied to some new way of doing things. The last major change was the Internet boom in the late 1990s. The, "But this time it is different" mantra was repeated because now people could buy things more efficiently; this was going to add value to everything we did. Investment analysts, mutual fund wholesalers, and clients all tried to rationalize to me why this change was the biggest thing ever. My response was historical fact. The railroads provided people the ability to travel faster and farther than a horse could carry them. This led to everyone wanting to own railroad stocks in the 1860s and 1870s. This wild enthusiasm for railroad stocks, of every kind, led to the railroad bust of 1873, which then led to the depression of 1873.

Cars and the radio were big changes in the 1920s. People thought these new industries were going to change the way we lived, and they did. They changed it so much that no price was too high to pay for any of the stocks; they were growing fast and were the future of the economy. RCA stock increased in value from 1925 to 1929 from around $20 per share to over $120 per share, RCA's stock price dropped to $5 after the crash of 1929. If you had been one of the people to invest in RCA before everyone was talking about it, you would have done just fine. However, if you had bought RCA stock after the big run up, you would have been waiting around over forty years just to break even.

When you hear that phrase, "But this time it's different" in regard to the high price of some investment, you know things are out of hand. We have seen it happen in the past, and it will happen at some time in the future. It is at times like these when people become most susceptible to greed.

One of the advisors in my firm received a call one day from a client. The client asked, "Shouldn't we pick up some Cisco?"

The advisor's response was, "Which one, the router company or the food company?"

The response was, "Whatever stock everyone is talking about."

By the way, Cisco's (the router company) stock went from over $80 to under $10 per share from 2000 to 2003.

Investment Strategy:

Most people treat investment planning the same way they treat retirement planning; they don't put as much thought into it as they should. With investing, you tend to have two camps. You have those willing to pay for advice and service, and you have the do-it-yourselfers.

Neither way is right or wrong; they are just two different approaches to accomplish the same things. If you do it yourself, you will need to study your portfolio. You will need a way to analyze it to make sure that you have an appropriate allocation, and that the investments are in line with your goals and risk tolerance. If you pay for service, you should not have to do this yourself. But, you do want to make sure that your advisor has the ability and knowledge to do this for you.

Let's start at the beginning. Whether you do it yourself or have an advisor, make sure you have an allocation that is appropriate for your goals, time horizon, and risk tolerance. Your portfolio's allocation will have more to do with your overall return than any other factor. It determines your portfolio's return far more than market timing or investment selection.

Let's think about it logically. If your allocation is 100 percent short-term C/Ds, then no matter how diligent you are shopping for high rates (and waiting for rates to rise) you will tend to average a low rate of return. Barring any wild jump in short-term interest rates, you will not earn over 6 percent return per year using this strategy. No matter how hard you work managing this portfolio over a twenty-year time frame, you would most likely under perform a diversified portfolio that includes both stocks and bonds.

On the other hand, based on your investment objectives and risk tolerance, you might average a higher rate of return if you invest entirely into a diversified portfolio of stocks over an extended period of time. Having a well diversified portfolio of different stock and bond categories will typically out-perform short-term bonds, and have less volatility than a portfolio invested in all stocks. It is true that poor investment selection and market timing can have an impact on your portfolio's performance, but your asset allocation will have a larger impact on how your portfolio performs than either.

The challenge of any asset allocation strategy is to have the discipline to stick with your allocation in good markets and bad. As I mentioned earlier, people tend to dramatically under-perform the market because they tend to buy high and sell low. If you have ever heard a report about mutual fund flows, you will see what I mean. Mutual fund flows track the money going into and out of different mutual funds. So, when someone says this fund had inflows of $100 million, that means this fund had $100 million more invested into it than it had taken out of it. When a fund has $100 million in outflows, this means people took out $100 million more than they had invested into this fund.

Janus Funds are an excellent example of this phenomenon. In

2000, the fund company had record inflows as people poured money into the hottest fund family of the 90s. When the tech bubble blew, the performance of the Janus funds dropped as well. Even though many of their funds started showing positive returns in 2003, the outflows continued. Their flagship fund, the Janus Fund, saw huge inflows in 2000 when its share price was over $40 per share. When the fund's share price bottomed out in 2003, there were record outflows for under $18 per share. This means people were anxious to put their money into the fund at $40 per share, and couldn't wait to get their money out at $18 per share. Logic should have told us we should have sold at $40 per share and then bought the fund back at $18, but that's not how human nature works.

The use of a disciplined investment allocation could have negated many of the losses that so many people suffered.

A disciplined asset allocation works like this; you allocate a specific percentage of your investments to a number of different asset classes. Each year you review this allocation to make sure you are not over-weighted in one asset class in relation to your personal objectives and risk tolerance. When you do your portfolio re-balance, you simply sell a portion of the asset class in which you are over-weighted (have too much invested) and buy some of the asset class in which you are under-weighted (don't have enough invested).

Here is an example. You develop an asset allocation that has 35 percent in government bonds, 10 percent in high yield bonds, 20 percent large cap stock, 10 percent small cap stock, 10 percent natural resources, and 15 percent international. After the first year of this allocation, let us assume that there has been a spike in inflation. Inflation will usually reduce the value of bonds and increase the value of natural resources. So, now you have 32 percent in government bonds, 8 percent in high-yield bonds, and 15 percent in natural resources. With the changes in the market values of some of the asset categories, you are now over-weighted in natural resources and under-weighted in bonds. You simply sell 3 percent of the natural resources fund and allocate that toward government bonds. You sell 2 percent of the natural resources and apply that towards the high-yield bonds. This simple illustration is not an actual case or a recommended allocation; it is simply a fictional example used to illustrate how this system works.

By rebalancing on a regular basis, you have accomplished two very important things. You have kept a disciplined allocation and you hopefully have bought low and sold high.

Keeping a disciplined allocation is important because asset values change. If you do not re-balance your portfolio from time to time, you might become over-weighted in an area where you don't want to be. This occurred to a number of people in the late 90s, when the stock market was setting new records.

Let's say you retired on January 1, 1995, with $1,000,000, and wanted to be conservative. You invest $300,000 into the stock market and invest the rest in high quality bonds, hoping to live off of the income that these bonds produce. You buy the bonds and start drawing off $50,000 per year interest. You invest the $300,000 into a fund that mimics the S&P 500 index. At the start of 2000, your bonds are still worth $700,000, but now your investment in an S&P 500 fund is worth over $1,000,000. That's not bad for six years. Your total account is now worth over $1,700,000 and things are looking bright. Do you remember what happens next? The market starts to drop, and by the end of 2002 your account is now down to about $1,250,000.

You might be thinking to yourself that this isn't bad, and you still have more in 2002 than when you started. This is true, but something else happened over that time frame; the interest rate you were receiving on your bonds dropped from 7.2 percent to around 4 percent. Now you would either start dipping into your principal, or convert your entire account into bonds in order to maintain your income. This doesn't even account for inflation.

Had you maintained your disciplined asset allocation, you would have much more invested in bonds and it would have been easier to maintain your income. You would not have seen your account go up nearly as much, but you wouldn't have seen it go down nearly as much either.

An added bonus to the disciplined allocation approach is that from 2000 to 2003, when the bonds were going up in value and the stocks were going down, you would have been taking profits in bonds and buying stocks. You would have been buying low and selling high.

Asset allocations are fairly easy to come by; many fund families offer asset allocation questionnaires that you can complete online, and they will generate a recommended allocation. Some fund companies can even do the allocation for you.

Many times you get what you pay for, but sometimes you don't. I have seen paid for asset allocation strategies that were not as thorough as allocation strategies they could have received for free from the Internet. So, go to a couple of different sources to compare their asset allocations. See which is the most thorough and has the best fit for you.

Just because you start with an appropriate asset allocation doesn't mean it will stay that way. Asset categories change over time. You will need to revisit the allocation at least once a year. Make certain it is still in balance and that you have an adequate source for your cash flow needs.

One of the primary benefits of having a disciplined asset allocation for your investments is predictability. When you know what the historical performance of an asset class is, and you know how much you are investing in that asset class, then you have a reasonable estimate of how that allocation will perform over time. Granted, you cannot accurately predict what your investments will do from day to day. But, over an extended period of time, each asset class's performance will typically fall into a range of returns. Since we know how much we are investing into each asset class, and know the historical ranges of each asset class, we can then predict with a reasonable degree of certainty what the portfolio's performance will be over a given period of time.

Please do not misunderstand what I am saying. I am not saying that anyone can predict how your portfolio will perform year-in and year-out. I am saying you can get a reasonable range of potential returns for the allocation you have selected. The range might be an upside of 25 percent and a downside of negative 10 percent for a one-year period. It might be an annual upside of 10 percent and a downside of negative 2 percent for a five-year period.

Knowing the range of performance is important, because it manages your expectations and makes you aware of the potential downside of your portfolio. It can also help you project how much income you can receive from your portfolio.

I feel that any good asset allocation analysis should include a probability model, often referred to as a Monte Carlo simulation. This is a statistical analysis of your portfolio. It will show the probability of your account remaining intact, over specific periods of time, given your anticipated distributions from your portfolio.

In 1999 and 2000, when many people wanted a 12 percent return or more on their retirement account, I would show them a very aggressive asset allocation. This allocation would be the most likely allocation to attain this 12 percent return for a ten-year period. Then, I would show historically how volatile this portfolio had been, and the probability that they would spend through all of their money. Many people didn't want to have the possibility of their accounts dropping over 35 percent in a single year, or the possibility of the account not showing a positive return for over fifteen years. Monte Carlo modeling, more than any other feature on my asset allocation tools, kept many people invested properly. And, this was during a period when many other investors were getting caught up in the irrational exuberance of a raging, bull market.

A disciplined asset allocation is exactly that, an allocation that is consistent through changing markets. Just because you use a broker or an advisor doesn't mean you will have a disciplined allocation. I remember sitting next to a broker; I could hear his conversations with clients, and many went something like this:

"Well, you have $100,000. To be properly diversified, I would suggest $20,000 in this fund, and $20,000 in that fund."

He would usually put people into five funds, with 20 percent in each fund. This approach is better than putting it all into one fund, but do not mistake it for a well-thought-out or well-designed asset allocation based on your situation and goals.

The reason this is not a well-thought-out asset allocation is because it is difficult to get proper diversification with five funds. One of the reasons you have an asset allocation is to help manage risk. So, no matter what the market or economic conditions are, you should, in theory, always have at least one investment or asset class that is doing well. How it works is very simple; there are some economic conditions that help out one asset class while hurting another. So, you might have one asset class performing well when another is performing poorly.

This is known as correlation; how assets correlate refers to how independent they are of one another. A high correlation between two asset classes means they tend to perform very similarly during changing market and economic conditions. A good example of this would be automakers; if you buy Ford and GM stock at the same time, you will find that they typically go up and down at the same time. The reason is that if auto sales are good for one company, they tend to be good for all. If expenses go up for one company, they tend to go up for all. I have seen brokers put people into eight different mutual funds they thought they were well diversified. Instead, every fund they owned was a large-cap value fund. You cannot be properly diversified if every fund you are invested in holds the same basic investments. If your funds have similar holdings and similar objectives, they will perform similarly to each other. In other words, when one fund is doing well they should all be doing well, and when one fund is doing poorly they should all be doing poorly.

You want your portfolio to contain assets that have a low, or negative, correlation to one another. For instance, a good asset class to offset the negative effects of the auto industry would be oil companies. Usually, higher oil prices hurt car manufacturers because people tend to buy smaller cars or have less to spend. Higher oil prices usually result in higher profits for oil companies, and therefore their stocks usually do well when oil prices rise. Another example would be companies affected by higher grain prices. Many times, when grain prices go up, the companies that make the seeds, chemicals, and equipment for the farmers do well. The companies that use that grain to make products to sell to the consumer usually don't do as well; they have to either raise their prices or receive less profit.

Why is this important? When putting together an asset allocation, you want to avoid having too many assets that will go up or down at the same time. If you are too heavily allocated in one type of investment, and that type of investment falls out of favor, where will you get your money when you need it? You will have to sell from an investment that is down in value.

Do you see how randomly picking investments would make it difficult to have a disciplined investment approach?

Let's say that you have five funds. Let's assume that you put 20 percent into large growth, 20 percent into large value, 20 percent into international, 20 percent into high-yield bonds and 20 percent into high-quality bonds.

This looks like a pretty good allocation, doesn't it? Given the limited number of funds you are invested in, this allocation will work well during a rising market or a market that is providing slow growth.

What happens if the global economy starts to slow down? If an economic slowdown occurs, four out of your five asset categories are probably not going to be performing well, because they are all tied to economic growth. Combine this with rising inflation, and you could have all five asset classes down at one time.

If you are drawing money out of your account, you now need to pull a higher percentage of your portfolio value just to maintain your current income.

Now, let's assume you have done a proper asset allocation. You have a bond ladder to fund your income needs; you have your assets invested in multiple asset categories that include natural resources, real estate, stocks, and bonds. Now, when a global economic slowdown occurs, even if every asset category you have is down, you still have bonds maturing every year to fund your income needs.

A quick comparison between the five-fund allocation, and a well-thought-out asset allocation, shows that by using correlation properly we can actually reduce the volatility of the portfolio while keeping the potential for growth. While diversification through an asset allocation strategy is a useful technique that can help to manage overall portfolio risk and volatility, there is no certainty or assurance that a diversified portfolio will enhance overall return or outperform one that is not diversified.

Let's go back to the broker I talked about earlier, the one who would put all of his clients in a five-fund portfolio. Instead of buying low and selling high, this broker would drop the worst performing fund in the portfolio and replace it with a better performing fund. This sounds very logical to most people. If you asked most investors if they wanted their funds managed in such a way, they would tend to say yes. But, lets look at what happens when your portfolio is managed in this manner.

We are going to assume that international under-performed the rest of the markets this year, and large-cap growth out-performed. In order to sell the loser and buy the winner, you need to get rid of your international exposure and buy another fund that performed well. Now you have 40 percent in large-cap growth and nothing in international. Let's assume that, in the next year, large-cap growth performs well again, and large-cap value under-performs. Now, you sell your large value and buy another large-cap growth fund. At the start of the third year, you have 60 percent of your entire portfolio in large-cap growth, 20 percent in high-yield bonds, and 20 percent in high-quality bonds. We know from past experience that trees don't grow to the sky, and returns tend to normalize over time. If this scenario looks familiar, remember back to the late 90s when large growth was the best performing asset class four years in a row. Then, in 2000, 2001, and 2002, large growth was one of the worst performing assets classes. By concentrating your portfolio in large-cap growth, using this strategy, you have over-weighted your portfolio into what will eventually under-perform other asset classes. Given this discipline, you would be completely out of large growth in 2002, just in time for a four-year rise in that asset class. You still have a discipline, but the discipline does not help you stay in a consistent allocation. Had you maintained the 20 percent in the five asset classes, which would mean selling a portion of the best performing funds and buying some of the worst performing funds, you would have been much better off when the market corrected. When you buy the best performer from last year, just because you want to be where people made money last year, you have lost your discipline.

Remember it is almost unheard of for a fund to be the best performer in its category two years in a row. It just doesn't happen. Usually, when a fund is the best performer in its category, people rush to put money into that fund. The fund managers have to figure out how to invest the huge flow of money coming into their fund. After they get the funds invested, if their performance is sub-par, they have to manage the huge amount of money flowing out of the fund. There are many examples of this happening to funds. People rush to put their money in the hot performer, and then rush to take it out when it is no longer the hot performer. We have seen it happen with real estate, technology, biotech, and oil; almost any industry you can think of has been the hot investment at one time or another.

When more money is going into a fund it is called inflows, or net inflows. When more money is leaving a fund than coming in it is known as outflows.

It is interesting to track inflows and outflows, because the better a fund is doing the more money tends to flow into that fund. The worse a fund is doing, the more outflows there tends to be. This means that people, as a rule, like to buy high and sell low. This explains why there is such a big difference between what the stock markets average performance is and the individual investors performance is.

A good way to remain disciplined is to have a written guideline for how you want your portfolio managed over time. This is often called an investment policy statement. An investment policy statement (IPS) is a tool used by many endowment funds, trusts, and pensions to establish a disciplined investment approach. An IPS simply states what percentage of the portfolio you plan to have allocated to each asset category, with what frequency the portfolio will be rebalanced, and if there are any investments that are prohibited. If you have a fee advisor, you should have an IPS to track how well the advisor is following the guidelines you have set forth for your portfolio. If you have a commission broker, they should be able to help you develop an IPS. Even if you are a do-it-yourselfer, you can develop your own IPS.

Set guidelines for your investment policy statement. Establish an investment selection criteria that specifically lays out what criteria a stock needs in order to qualify. If your selection criterion is any stock on your brokerage firm's buy list, you might want to rethink how you pick your stocks. The problem with using a buy list of stocks from a brokerage firm, is that you might wind up over-allocated to a specific industry or style. You also don't want to say that the best performing mutual fund in each asset class is what you want to invest in, because this fund will change every year. You want to have a disciplined, rational approach to your investment selection.

If you work with an advisor or a broker, ask them for their investment selection criteria.

Once you have established how you are going to select your investments, you need to establish how you are going to allocate those investments. Establish your asset allocation based on your time horizon, income needs, and risk tolerance.

Now that you have an appropriate allocation established, decide how often you are going to rebalance it. You will not want to micromanage the account and rebalance daily or weekly. Decide if you will rebalance the portfolio one, two, or four times each year. Whatever rebalance you decide to use, stick to it. You don't want to change this discipline just because the market is headed up or down.

Do not change your allocation to more conservative when the market goes down, and more aggressive when the market goes up. This is human nature, and it is a hard temptation to avoid. If you do this, you are buying high and selling low. We don't want to do that because we want to buy low and sell high.

Review the IPS once a year to make sure it is still appropriate, and make changes if needed.

Before you implement your plan and make the investments, you want to do a Monte Carlo model to make sure that your income expectations are realistic for your allocation.

Once you have selected what investments you want to invest in, and you have your asset allocation and investment policy statement, you need to have a system to figure your investment performance.

Why do you need to have a way to figure investment performance? How are you going to know how well you are doing if you can't figure out the annual performance of your account? You cannot allow your memory to keep track of how much you started with, how much you have withdrawn, and what return you have averaged since the inception of the portfolio.

When asking someone how their portfolio has done over a given period of time, most people will either overestimate or underestimate the amount of return they have received by a long shot.

I met with one person who thought their account had done almost nothing for ten years. After analyzing their performance, and showing them their results, they were very pleased. I met with another person who thought their account had done great. After analyzing their results, they were not happy at all. The first person thought they had started out with almost twice the amount of money than they actually had. The second person's account returned a little over 4 percent average, even though they were invested 100 percent in stocks and the stock market had averaged over 10 percent during the same time frame.

The fact that we tend to remember things differently than they actually happened is why it is so important to be able to track the performance of your portfolio. This way, you actually know how well your investments have done.

Why is it so important to be able to track the performance of your portfolio? If the investments you are in consistently under perform, then you have less money to live on. I have had some people argue that their fund underperforms on the upside, but doesn't seem to go down as much on the down side. This may be true in some cases, but not always. I have seen funds that have not gone up nearly as much as similar funds when the market was rising. However, they dropped just as much as other funds when the market dropped.

Performance is never as straightforward as it seems. I was at an event, and a gentleman came up to me with a great deal of pride. He said, "My international fund went up 13 percent last year; can you beat that?""

I didn't have the heart to tell him that the EAFE index, which is a developed-market international index, was up over 20 percent for the same period. If all you do is look at performance, and don't compare it to anything, you cannot judge if you are doing well or doing poorly. It is like saying, "It only took me eight hours to get to New York."

Is eight hours a good time in which to get to New York? It depends; did you drive or fly, and do you live in New Jersey or California? Depending where you are and what mode of transportation you take makes the difference as to whether eight hours is making good time or horrible time. You should compare your investment's results to an index that most closely resembles your investment. That way, you will know how well you have done.

Then, the man asked if I thought now was a good time to put more money into this fund. How do you respond to a question like that? You should never think that because an investment did well last year, you should put more money into it now. My response to him was, "It depends on your current allocation, your risk tolerance, time horizon, and expectations for this money."

He had never thought about having some rationale for making an investment decision. Like most people, he wanted to put more money into the asset class that was performing the best.

There are two things to consider with this example. Was the fund's performance good for the risk he was taking, and was this an appropriate investment for this person's allocation?

In the example above, this person's investment might not be that closely correlated to the EAFE index. In other words, when the EAFE index goes down 10 percent, maybe his fund only dropped 2 percent. If this were the case, his fund is probably more conservative than the EAFE index; that would explain why it underperformed when the index was going up. If his fund went down as much as the EAFE index in a bad market, and then underperformed when the market went up, he is taking the same risk but not getting the same upside potential. If you are going to take the risk for loss, you might as well get the potential upside.

A good way to compare this is standard deviation. Standard deviation is a calculation that assigns a risk number to a fund based on the fund's variation of returns. So, if you have a fixed C/D or annuity that has no variable in its performance, this investment would have a standard deviation close to zero. If you have an investment that is an aggressive growth, your standard deviation could be as high as twenty.

Beta is simply a volatility measure. Most betas are based on a comparison to the S&P 500 index. So, if you are looking at a fund and it has a beta of 0.5, that means that it tends to move up and down half as much as the S&P 500. If the beta is 1.25, that means it tends to be 25 percent more volatile than the S&P 500. Be careful with beta; a low beta doesn't necessarily mean low volatility, it just means it doesn't fluctuate the same way the S&P 500 index does. International funds that tend to have high standard deviations (meaning they are more volatile) can have low betas because they do not fluctuate at the same time that the S&P 500 index does. Make sure the beta is relevant; if you are looking at an international fund, it would make more sense to compare it's volatility to the EAFE index than the S&P 500.

Using standard deviation to monitor your investments is really quite easy; you compare your fund's standard deviation to that of a comparable index. If your fund and the index have very similar standard deviation numbers, you are taking similar risk to that of the index. If the investment objectives are the same, then you should have similar performance as well. If your performance is lower than the index, you might want to see what other funds are available within the same investment category.

When looking at performance, don't think all stocks are going to perform equally. Stocks move up and down based on investor sentiment. In the late 90s, when everything was Internet, the technology companies involved. were mostly large-cap growth and small-cap growth; their stocks were going through the roof. These stocks were offering annual returns in excess of 30 percent per year from 1995 to 1999. At the same time, small-cap value stocks were dropping 5 percent per year. This was because many people felt that value stocks were never going to perform as well as growth stocks. Investors would sell their value stocks in order to put their money into growth stocks.

After several years of this, the people who were interested in owning growth stocks already had their money invested into growth stocks. Do you know what usually happens when everyone who can buy growth stocks already owns all they want? Once there is no new money flowing into an investment, the potential for an increase in that investment's price is limited.

When there are tremendous inflows into a specific asset category, it can cause that asset category to outperform other asset classes. Large-cap stocks can outperform small-cap stocks if large-cap stocks are in favor. Other times, growth stocks outperform value stocks. There are even times when different stock categories perform similarly to each other.

What you want to avoid is getting caught up in the hysteria of putting your investments into an asset class just because everyone else is doing it. Stay disciplined and stick with your asset allocation.

A good way to measure your investment's performance is to

compare them to an equivalent index, so you are comparing apples to apples. You should also consider whether your portfolio is mostly stocks or mostly bonds. You do not want to compare your bond portfolio to the S&P 500 index, just like you wouldn't want to compare your stock portfolio to the Barclay's bond index, or any other non-equity related index.

You can look at Lipper averages to compare your portfolio's performance results with that of an average, balanced fund. The main problem here is that the actively managed funds that make up the average might not correspond well with your particular portfolio. They can, however, give you a fairly close representation of your portfolio's performance compared to what the average professional money manager's performance was for the same time period. Here is where it gets a little bit tricky; you need to figure out what Lipper index your portfolio most closely resembles. These indices are a useful tool to track the performance of your portfolio, but matching your allocation to the correct index isn't as easy as it sounds. The Lipper indexes are not as easy to find as the S&P 500 or the Barclay's bond index.

So, if you are willing to do a little math, here is a good solution for you. Depending on your stock allocation, you can select an appropriate index. If you have a well-diversified stock portfolio covering all asset classes, the Wilshire 5000 might be a good fit for you. But, this index is not as easy to find as many of the other major indexes. If you only have large-cap stocks, the S&P 500 might be the best fit; it is very easy to find performance numbers for the S&P 500. You can usually find what type of investments, and the investment parameters of the corresponding index, by doing a little research in order to see if an index is a good fit for your comparisons.

Bonds are very similar, if you only invest in Treasury bonds, there is a Treasury index. If you have a diversified bond portfolio, you can use the Barclay's composite bond index. This index uses multiple types of bonds with many different maturities.

For simplicity's sake, we will assume that you have a well-diversified bond and stock portfolio. Thus, we will use the Wilshire 5000 and the Barclay's US aggregate index.

In this example, let's assume you have 50 percent in stocks and 50 percent in bonds, and your portfolio yielded a 7 percent return last year. Was this good performance or not? On average, 7 percent on a conservative allocation looks pretty good to me. But, let's compare it to the indexes to see how you did on a relative basis.

To compare your portfolio's performance to the indexes performance, all we need to do is take the percentage of your account that is allocated to stocks and multiply it by the return of the Wilshire 5000. Then, we take the percentage you have allocated to bonds and multiply that by the return of the Barclay's bond index. Once you have done that, you simply add the two numbers together. Then you can compare your portfolio's return to the major indexes.

Let's assume the Wilshire 5000 was up 10 percent, and the Lehman Aggregate was up 6 percent. Since we have 50 percent in stocks, and 50 percent in bonds, you simply take 10 percent (the return of the Wilshire 5000) times 50 percent (the percentage of the portfolio invested in stocks). This gives you 5 percent. Now we do the same thing with the bond portion of the portfolio. Since we have 50 percent of the portfolio in bonds, we simply take 6 percent (the return from the Lehman Brothers Aggregate) times 50 percent (the percentage of the portfolio invested in bonds) and this gives you 3 percent. Now, you add the stock percentage (5 percent) to the bond percentage (3 percent) and this gives you 8 percent.

Your portfolio returned 7 percent, whereas the indexes returned 8 percent.

So, your mathematical formula would look like this:

(Percentage of portfolio invested in stocks times the return for the appropriate index) + (percentage of portfolio invested in bonds times the return of the appropriate index) = the equivalent allocated index return.

In the example above, the appropriate allocated index returned 8 percent, and your portfolio returned 7 percent. You did lag behind the index, but not by a substantial margin; I wouldn't make any drastic changes because of this difference. You will have years that you lag behind the indexes, and years that you outperform the indexes. Hopefully you will outperform more than lag.

You might be thinking to yourself that this seems like a lot of work just to see how your investments are doing. Why would I go to this much trouble just to see how well or poorly I am doing?

For the first part, this really doesn't take much time. If you have access to the Internet, you can simply Google the terms "Wilshire 5000 December performance report 2007," or whichever year you are comparing. Then, do the same with the Lehman bond aggregate. Google "Lehman aggregate bond performance," and you should be able to find the performance numbers. Most libraries will have financial resources that can provide that information to you.

If you have an account with a professional money manager, or an advisor that is charging a fee, they usually provide some type of comparison data on the performance reports.

If you currently do not get this type of information from your broker/advisor, ask them if they could provide it to you. If they are unable or unwilling to provide this type of service for you, make sure that they have low fees. The reason I say this, is because you are doing part of their job. If you are doing some of their work, you should get a discount.

We compare our car's gas mileage with equivalent cars. If our car is getting ten miles to the gallon, and someone else has a similar car that gets thirty miles to the gallon, we are going to take it somewhere to find out why our car is doing so poorly.

Why don't we pay as close attention to our investments as we do our gas mileage? How much do you spend a year in gas? How much do you lose each year by being invested in an inefficient portfolio? I am willing to bet that you have much more at stake with your investments than you do your car.

Reviewing your portfolio and making necessary changes takes more effort than doing nothing; this is true. But, if you don't maintain your portfolio and you wind up running out of money, the few hours it would have taken to monitor and review your portfolio each year will look like a very small price to pay.

This is portfolio maintenance. Just like maintaining a car is important, maintaining your portfolio is important as well. It is easier to let things go, but things tend to work better when they are well maintained. Consider a garden, if you want results in your garden, you can either hire someone to maintain it, or you can do it yourself. But, for you to have a successful garden it needs to be maintained.

Just like a flower garden needs to have a variety of plants and flowers, your portfolio needs to have a variety of investments. If you have ever made several trips to a botanical garden or park, over the course of one year, you can see what I mean. Most likely, this botanical garden or park has a beautiful flowerbed. The flowerbed usually doesn't just look nice one season of the year; this is because they are usually planted so they have some colorful blooms throughout the year. Just like areas that are heavy in tulips and daffodils will bloom early in the spring, areas with roses and lilies will be in bloom later.

If you do not realize that tulips and daffodils will not bloom in the summer, you might be disappointed when you go back to see these beautiful flowers in June and there are none to be seen. A good allocation should work the same way; throughout market changes you should have some investments that are doing well while other investments might not do as well. Bonds tend to perform better than stocks when the economy is slowing down; stocks tend to outperform bonds when the economy is doing well. If the economy is growing, you would expect your stocks to do well. So, in a good economy, you would expect a portfolio that is heavily allocated to bonds to under perform a stock portfolio. When the economy is in recession, a bond portfolio should outperform a stock portfolio.

Due to the fact that economists cannot accurately predict a recession until we are practically in one, it makes sense to have a diversified portfolio.

I learned a long time ago that nobody knows what the market will do from day to day or year to year. People make great livings trying to predict which way the market will go; some are better than others but nobody knows for certain how the markets will perform or which sectors will be the best performing.

I have known people who listened to an expert regarding which way the market was going to move. If this person said the market was going to drop, they wanted to sell everything they had. If this person said the market was going to go up, they wanted to buy more stocks. This particular expert started out with very good predictions regarding the market direction, but after a few years he tended to be wrong much more than right.

I bring this up because so many people want to have a magic formula to predict how the market will perform. Individuals and companies are all too happy to oblige. At any given time you can see or hear hundreds of predictions regarding market performance. Some will be right and others will be wrong. The problem is, we will not know which one is right or wrong until after the fact.

If you rely on experts to get in and out of the market, I am afraid you will be disappointed. If they knew when to get in and out of stocks, these experts would have so much money they wouldn't need to sell their advice to anyone willing to buy it.

One of the few tools I saw that actually did a good job in predicting market direction was on *Wall Street Week* with Louis Rukeyser.

He had a chart that compared financial newsletter writer's views on the market. When a majority of these people who wrote newsletters felt the market was going to go up, the market would usually go down. When a majority of these writers thought the market was going to go down, it usually went up.

One of the best examples of this was back in 1991. The Gulf War was about to start, and almost every analyst predicted that once the shooting started the markets would have a huge drop. Well, the shooting started and the market had one of its largest percentage gains in history. If you had been sitting on the sidelines, waiting for the drop, you would have missed a very big gain. The reason is because when everyone thinks the market is going to drop, everyone who wants out of the market is already out. Who is going to sell to push the market down further? When everyone thinks the market is going up, anyone who wants to be in the market is already in. Who is going to buy to push the market up?

The bottom line is that there is no magic formula; the experts don't know exactly what the market will do from year to year. The best way to manage your portfolio is to have an appropriate allocation and be disciplined to stick with it. Don't just jump from one allocation to another.

I think I have discussed this topic enough; it is an important topic, and something that many people often mess up.

CHAPTER 12
Retirement in a Nutshell

Retirement is as individual as you are. Nobody can engineer your retirement unless they know you extremely well. A person who has never met you, who has no idea what your plans are, is not able to give you advice about your retirement planning. When you see an expert talking about how much you need to have saved before you retire, they might be completely off base. The people we see telling us that we need to have 60 to 70 percent of our current income when we retire are talking about a percentage of retirees; you may or may not fit into this group.

When a major league baseball player gets up to bat, it is a good bet they will make an out, two out of three times. So, if you were going to make a prediction you could say, "He's not going to get a hit." But, what fun would the game be if you were always right and no one ever got a hit? So, when someone is talking about the percentage of income you will need to retire, they are talking about the majority of retirees. This may not include you.

Calculate all of the money you will make each year when you retire. Just because you can earn 75 percent of your current income when you retire, you can't just assume that it is okay to go ahead and retire. You will want to make sure that you will be able to do everything that is important to you.

There are two ways to analyze your retirement; these are the top-down and bottom-up approaches. The top-down approach is where you figure out how much money you will have from all sources when you retire, and you then figure out what things you will be able to do with those funds. You prioritize the things you want to do, and allocate your funds accordingly.

The bottom-up approach is where you figure out what you want to do in retirement, and then plan how much money you need to accomplish this.

The top-down approach usually works better if you are retiring sooner than you had expected. Because you are prioritizing, the things you want to do are based on the amount of money you have to spend. This way, you can focus on what is most important to you.

The bottom-up approach works best when you have flexible retirement plans. You figure out the things you want to spend your money on when you retire, such as a vacation home, RV, or travel. Then, you figure out how much money you need to have in order to accomplish this. So, if you do not have enough money to do everything you really want to do once you retire, you simply work a little longer to accumulate more money.

If you started out with the bottom-up approach and decided that you didn't have enough money to do all the things you really wanted to do, but you don't want to work anymore, you switch to the top-down approach. This allows you to prioritize what you want to do with the money you have available.

Do you retire as soon as possible and struggle financially for the next thirty years through retirement? Do you work for the next twenty-five years and leave a bunch of money to someone because you never spent it? Or, do you plan and save so you can spend as many years as possible doing what you really want to do? These are questions that only you can answer.

Once you know what you want to do once you retire, and how

much money it will take for you to live the retirement you have always dreamed of, make sure that you have your spending under control. If you spend a lot of time shopping or gambling, make sure these are not addictions that will deplete your life savings.

Once you retire, you will have more time on your hands to shop or gamble. What used to be a pastime that didn't cost much, because you didn't have much time to do it, could become quite costly when you have more time.

Though your children might be grown, that doesn't mean they are weaned. If you have adult children who are not financially self-sufficient, you might want to make sure they become self-sufficient before you retire. I have seen this happen many times. A parent retires, receives a large, pension, rollover check, and winds up spending it on their kids. You didn't work all of those years to wind up broke in retirement. After you run out of money, will your children finally become financially responsible?

If you have a child who is suffering through financial hardship, this is one of the hardest things you will have to deal with. Saying no to a child in need is hard. What will happen to your child if they still need money and now you are broke too?

If you haven't already done so, start an exercise program to help you stay fit, mobile, and active once you retire.

Figure out what your hobbies will be, so your mind stays sharp and you will have something you enjoy doing when you have some spare time. This also helps prevent you from getting roped into something you don't want to do.

The final thing to do is either have a competent financial advisor, or become well educated on managing your investments. This will help you have a reasonable expectation about how much money you can take from your savings and investments. Having knowledge of the risks associated with investing can help you manage your risks in all types of investing. Remember, the stock market is not the only risk you face. There is also credit risk, in case your investment goes bankrupt, and purchasing power risk, in case your earnings don't keep up with inflation.

Managing your assets includes monitoring performance, as well as establishing and maintaining a rationale investment allocation. If your current broker or advisor does not have a rationale investment allocation for your circumstances, then you need to establish one. If you have no way to track your portfolio's performance, relative to a relevant index, then you need to create a way to track your performance.

Monitor and review your portfolio annually so that you can track the performance of your portfolio; this will ensure that you are able to maintain your standard of living. Adjust as necessary, either the allocation or your standard of living.

The final area I want to cover is the idea of your house as a retirement vehicle. It is true that many people's largest asset is their house. It is also true that when you retire your house can be a source of income if needed.

One fallacy I have heard time and time again is that the larger, more expensive house that you buy, the more you will have when you retire. So, buy the largest, most expensive house you can buy while you are working. The problem with this notion is that, in order for you to have this large, expensive house, you have to pay for it. The larger the house you buy, the more furniture you will need. The taxes will be higher and the home will cost more to maintain.

This theory of putting a lot of money into your house is based on the idea that you are using someone else's money, and your house will appreciate to be worth much more than you paid for it.

It is true that you will be using someone else's money, at least if you borrow to buy the house. It is not necessarily true that the house will appreciate in value. Historically, houses have appreciated over long periods of time, but there are times when houses have actually lost value. During the Great Depression, many people who bought large houses when times were good could not sell them when times got bad. Instead of paying the taxes on a house, many would simply tear down their house so they could keep the lot.

I don't expect this type of thing to happen again. But, if you are relying on your house to provide income for retirement, and it's value is much less than you expected, it could hurt your retirement.

After taxes, interest, and expenses, most people merely break even on their house. It works to accumulate money because you are forced to make the payments. If you were forced to put money into an S&P 500 index fund every month for thirty years, you would be amazed at how much money you would have by the end of that period.

If you are looking to compare the cost of your mortgage, you can go to my website: www.montgomeryinvest.com. Find the financial calculator section so you can see what your loan payoff would be.

You now have more options than ever to get money out of your house. It used to be that if you needed the house to provide money for your living needs, you would either sell it or rent it out. Now they have home equity loans and reverse mortgages.

I do not have an opinion if either of these are good or bad; I just want to give you a simple explanation as to how they work.

Let's start off with the home equity loan, or a home equity line of credit. You simply use the equity in your house as collateral with a bank in order to get a loan. The equity you currently have in your house is simply the difference between what your house is worth and what you owe on it.

Many people have these types of credit arrangements. I have a line of credit with a checkbook. Anytime I need to use my line of credit, I just write a check. A home equity loan is where you go to the bank and you take out a loan. For most cases, the line of credit works better because you are only borrowing the money you need at that point in time.

If you have not paid the loan or line of credit off when you go to sell the house, you simply take the proceeds from the sale of your house to pay back what you owe.

Houses are a great way to build net worth, but don't think that buying a larger house automatically means more money in retirement.

Thank you for reading my book; I hope you found it beneficial.

I hope you have a long, happy, healthy, and rewarding retirement.

CHAPTER 13
Glossary-Key Terms

Many of these terms will have multiple meanings; I am simply providing the meaning that I feel is the closest representation to the terms used in regard to the financial services market. Any tax or legal definitions should not be considered a recommendation in any way, shape, or form. Please consult your appropriate advisor if you have any questions on how these definitions might relate to your specific situation.

Actively Managed Funds: Actively managed funds are mutual funds that have a portfolio manager who buys and sells investments to achieve a particular goal, such as exceeding the return of a relevant index or benchmark. These funds generally have more buy and sell activity than passively managed funds, whose objective is to mirror the performance of a particular index by purchasing the stocks included in that index.

Aggressive Investment Posture: An asset mix that has relatively more risk, but has the potential to provide higher potential returns with greater uncertainty. Aggressive asset mixes do not always produce higher returns than more conservative asset mixes.

Asset Allocation: The process of spreading assets among different asset classes such as stocks, bonds, and cash to help manage risk and reward.

Asset Class: A standard term that broadly defines a category of potential investments, such as stocks, bonds and cash.

Asset Mix: The percentage weightings (or mix) of different asset classes to be held in the portfolio.

Balanced Fund: A mutual fund that invests in stocks and bonds in an effort to provide both income and capital appreciation. Its purpose is to provide the investor with a fund that can provide both income and growth potential.

Bond: Also known as a "debt instrument," is a loan that an investor makes to an entity—the U.S. government, a municipality or corporation—in exchange for interest payments. The investor receives the principal back at the end of the bond term, which is usually ten, twenty, or thirty years.

Brokerage Account: An account held at a brokerage firm. Most brokerage accounts can hold stocks, bonds, mutual funds, and other types of securities.

Call Feature: A call feature is associated with bonds. A call feature is an option the issuer places on the bond that allows them to redeem or "call back" the bond prior to its maturity date. This usually occurs when the issuer is able to re-issue the debt at a lower interest rate.

Cash or Cash Equivalents: Investments of high liquidity that can easily be converted into cash. Money market funds and Treasury Bills are examples.

Certificates Of Deposit (CDs): CDs are interest-bearing, FDIC insured debt instruments issued by banks with maturities from a few months to several years.

Closed-End Fund: Closed-end funds are mutual funds that have a fixed number of shares outstanding and trade on an exchange, similar to an individual stock. They tend to be actively managed and can sell at a discount or premium to their underlying net asset value.

Commodities: Commodities are physical substances, such as oil, corn, or copper that are usually traded in the form of futures contracts.

Conservative Investment Posture: Asset mixes that have relatively low risk in general will often also have lower, long-term returns than more aggressive asset mixes.

Consumer Price Index/CPI: The Consumer Price Index (CPI) is an inflationary indicator that measures the change in the cost of a fixed basket of differently weighted goods and services, such as food, electricity and housing that are used by an average family of four located in a major metropolitan area in the U.S. The Social Security cost of living adjustment is based on changes to the CPI.

Contingent Deferred Sales Charge (CDSC): This is also known as a back-end sales charge. It is a sales charge levied when the investment, such as a mutual fund or annuity, is sold during a predetermined timeframe.

Corporate Bonds: Debt instruments issued by a corporation, as distinct from ones issued by a government agency or municipality. They are taxable, with a par value of $1,000, a specific maturity date, and can usually be bought or sold on the open market. They also tend to have higher interest rates than government bonds as they tend to carry more risk.

Derivatives: Are a financial contract whose values are derived from the value of an underlying security or indicator, such as options and commodities futures contracts. Derivatives may be used for hedging purposes or speculation.

Dow Jones Industrial Average (DJIA): The DJIA is a price-weighted index comprised of thirty of the largest and most widely held stocks in the United States. Editors of the Wall Street Journal decide which stocks are to be added and which stocks are to be dropped.

EAFE Index—Eupore, Australasia and Far East: Is an unmanaged, market value-weighted index produced by Morgan

Stanley to measure the overall performance of the international markets of developed countries.

Emerging Markets: Emerging market securities invest in stocks in developing (emerging) countries throughout the world. This requires an investor to be alert to the possibly illiquid markets and movements in foreign currencies. These investments are considered to be more aggressive and may contain more risk than investments in developed countries.

Equities/Stocks: A stock is an ownership or equity stake in a corporation. There are many factors that can impact a stock's price. If the company does well in its industry, then the stock price may go up and the company may issue dividends to shareholders. On the other hand, if the company is less profitable in comparison to its peers, then investors might sell the stock, which can in turn lower the stock's price.

Exchange Traded Fund (ETFs): Exchange traded funds track an index. These funds trade on an exchange like an individual stock, even though they may bundle many different issues that are in the index it tracks. An exchange-traded fund's performance should track fairly closely the index that they represent. ETFs can represent stocks, bonds, or commodities. ETFs do not have an Net Asset Value (NAV) like most mutual funds; their price fluctuates like a stock and can be bought and sold at any time.

Fixed Annuities: Financial contract between an individual and an insurance company. The individual gives the insurance company money in exchange for periodic lifetime payments at a later date. A fixed immediate annuity offers fixed payments immediately, either for life or for a specified period.

Futures: Futures are a standardized contract to buy/sell a specific amount of a commodity/financial instrument at a given price on a future date.

General Partnership: An association that has been created by an agreement by multiple persons ("partners") and has all partners personally liable for all debts and/or legal actions against the company. Partners are liable for all debts/liabilities of the company, not only the ones they incur on behalf of the company. Partners share in the profits and losses of the partnership. As a general partner, your losses can exceed your initial investment.

Growth Stocks: Growth stocks are shares in a company whose earnings are expected to grow at an above-average rate relative to the market. Small cap, mid-cap or large cap stocks can also be "growth" stocks.

Hedging: Hedging is a method of protecting an investment from adverse market movement. Hedging can be done through direct investment or the purchase of futures or options (derivatives) that would consist of taking an offsetting position of one currently owned.

High-Yield Bonds: A bond that is issued by organizations that has a lower than "investment grade" credit rating. These bonds will generally pay a higher interest rate (yield) to compensate for the greater risk the investor takes.

Index: An index is a statistical indicator that provides a representation of the values of the securities within the index. Examples: S&P 500, Dow Jones Industrial Average, EAFE, the UK's FTSE 100 and France's CAC 40.

Indexing: Indexing is a method of investing in a similar proportion to an underlying index. This is usually done by investing in Exchange Traded Funds (ETFs) or Index Mutual Funds which are held for a long period of time and designed to "match" the market, not beat it. This type of investing is sometimes called "Passive Investing" due to its buy and hold nature.

Individual Retirement Account (IRA): IRA is an account that allows investment dollars to grow tax deferred. There are two main types of IRA accounts: Traditional and Roth. In the case of a Roth

IRA, deposits into the account are done on an after-tax basis and proceeds can be withdrawn tax free if certain provisions are met. Roth IRA contributions are not tax deductible. A Traditional IRA allows assets to grow tax deferred and may allow for contributions to be deducted from your taxes if you qualify. Distributions are usually taxed as ordinary income and, if taken before age fifty-nine-and-a-half may require an income tax penalty to be paid. A self-directed IRA is an account that allows you to select the investments that will be placed in the IRA. An IRA rollover is the process of moving assets from a qualified retirement plan into an IRA.

Inflation Adjusted Dollars: The value of an asset measured in terms of future purchasing power. Because of inflation (increase in the cost of goods and services), today's dollars will probably not be able to buy as much in the future as they can today.

Intermediate Term Government Bonds: Debt securities issued by the U.S. government or federal agencies that have a maturity of two to ten years.

International Bonds: Bonds issued by a non-domestic entity.

International (Foreign) Equities: Securities of foreign corporations.

Investment Grade Bonds: Municipal or corporate bonds that are generally judged by the ratings agencies as having a relatively lower risk of default.

Large Cap Stocks: Equity securities of large-capitalization companies. Large-cap stocks generally have a market capital in excess of $5 billion.

Leverage: Leverage is typically using debt to increase your equity position. A leveraged fund has borrowed money to increase the amount it can invest into a particular investment.

Limited Partnership: A partnership between two or more persons with at least one General Partner and one Limited Partner. Limited partnerships have a general partner that is responsible for the operation of the partnership, and have unlimited liability. Limited partners who have rights to the partnership's cash flow and are liable only up to the extent of their investment.

Long-Term Government Bonds: Debt securities issued by the U.S. government or federal agencies that have a maturity of more than ten years

Buying on Margin: Buying on margin is a manner of using borrowed money from the broker/dealer where the account is held in order to purchase securities. The collateral for the loan is the other securities in the account. The investor uses the assets inside of a brokerage account as collateral to borrow funds.

Market Capitalization: Market capitalization refers to the aggregate value of a particular company or stock. How you calculate a company's market cap is by multiplying the total shares outstanding by the stock's current price per share.

Mid-Cap Stocks: Equity securities of medium-sized capitalization companies. A mid-cap stock will have a market capitalization of $2 to $5 billion.

Mortgage-Backed Securities: Debt obligations that represent claims to the cash flows from pools of mortgage loans, most commonly on residential properties. Most mortgage backed securities are issued by the Federal Home Loan Mortgage Corporation (FHLMC), the Government National Mortgage Association (GNMA) or the Federal National Mortgage Association (FNMA), US Government sponsored enterprises. Investors are generally entitled to a pro-rata share of the principal and interest payments made on the pool of loans.

Municipal Bonds: Debt obligation of a state or local government entity. The funds may support general government needs or special projects. Interest income is exempt from federal income taxes, and in some cases, from state and local taxes.

Mutual Fund: Mutual funds are a pool of funds collected from many investors with the purpose of investing in securities. Mutual funds are professionally managed by money managers who attempt to produce capital gains for its investors. A mutual fund can invest in stocks, bonds, commodities, etc.

Net-Asset Value (NAV): A mutual fund's price per share or an ETF's per-share value. It is calculated by dividing the total value of assets less any liabilities by the number of shares outstanding.

Non-Qualified Assets: Non-qualified assets are not part of an exempt fund such as an IRA, 401(k) plan or other employer sponsored defined contribution plan. Income received from assets held in a non qualified account are subject to federal, state, and local taxes.

Par Value: The nominal dollar value assigned to a security by the issuer. For debt securities, par is the amount paid to the investor at maturity, generally $1,000 on a corporate bond.

Passive Investing: Investing in securities for the long-term, limiting buy and sell actions. Known as a buy and hold approach.

Price/Earnings Ratio (P/E RATIO): Price to earnings ratio is a valuation ratio of the current share price of a company divided by its earnings per share. Generally, a higher P/E ratio suggests that investors are anticipating higher earnings growth in the future.

Private Equity Firms: An investment manager that raises pools of money (private equity funds) to invest in the private equity of a company. Private equity firms earn a periodic management fee along with a share in the profits earned from each private equity fund managed.

Qualified Assets: Qualified assets are held within a certain type of account such as an IRA, 401(k) plan or other employer sponsored defined contribution plan. These assets are allowed to accumulate tax-deferred inside of the qualified plan. These assets will be taxed as ordinary income when the funds are withdrawn from the plan, provided the participant is over age fifty-nine-and-a-half. Otherwise, withdrawals may be subject to penalties in addition to paying ordinary income taxes.

Rate of Return/ROR Or Return on Investment/ROI: A performance measure that is used to evaluate an investments efficiency and generally expressed as a percentage. It is calculated by dividing the return (gain-capital invested) by the capital invested. Example: Capital investment is $100, value is currently $110. ROR = 110-100/100 x 100 = 10%

Real Estate Investment Trust (REIT): A security that sells like a stock on major exchanges and invests directly in real estate through real property or mortgages or a combination of both. A REIT will get preferential tax treatment in return for certain considerations, the biggest being that it must pay out at least 90 percent of profits as dividends. REITs can be either publicly or privately held.

Risk: The quantifiable likelihood of loss or less than expected investment returns.

Sales Charge (LOAD): The sales charge is the fee associated with the purchase or sale of a mutual fund or variable annuity. Front-end loads are paid as part of the purchase where a back-end load is paid at the time of sale.

Small Cap Stocks: Equity securities that have a small-market capitalization, small-cap stocks generally have a market capital of between $300 million and $2 billion.

Speculation: Taking a high degree of risk on the purchase of an investment with the intentions of profit from anticipated price movements.

Standard and Poor's 500 (S&P 500): A market-weighted index made up of 500 large-cap stocks that indicate the broad moves of the stock market.

Stock Exchange: A place where shares of stock or stock equivalents are traded. An exchange can be a physical location, like the

New York Stock Exchange, or electronic, like the NASDAQ.

Stock Market: A generic and broad definition for the organized trading of stocks through the exchanges or over-the-counter markets.

Time Value of Money: Represents the concept that money has different values depending on when it is received. For example, because of inflation, which causes the value of goods and services to increase, a dollar today may be worth less than a dollar in the future because its purchasing power is depleted by the amount of inflation.

Total Return: The combined return in income (through dividends and interest) and capital appreciation/depreciation of the price from an investment over a given time period.

T-Bills/Treasury Bills: T-Bills are negotiable debt obligations issued by the U.S. government and backed by its full faith and credit, with maturities of one year or less. They are typically issued at a discount and mature at par value.

T-Notes/Treasury Notes: T-Notes are negotiable debt obligations issued by the U.S. government and backed by its full faith and credit, with maturities of between one and ten years.

Treasury Bonds: Treasury bonds are negotiable, coupon-bearing debt obligations issued by the U.S. government and backed by its full faith and credit, with maturities over seven years, but generally fall between ten and thirty years. These bonds pay interest every six months at a fixed coupon rate.

Trusts (Revocable and Irrevocable): A revocable trust is a trust that can be altered or terminated during the grantor's lifetime. Since the trust can be altered during the grantor's lifetime, the assets contained in the trust are considered part of the grantor's estate for estate tax purposes. The assets are only passed on to the beneficiaries after the grantor's death, and at that time, the trust becomes irrevocable. An irrevocable trust is a trust where the provisions cannot be changed under normal circumstances (the beneficiary has to agree) until the trust has expired or its purpose completed.

Value Stocks: Value stocks can have characteristics such as low price-earnings ratio, low price-book ratio and/or high dividend yield. They generally trade lower than their fundamentals, i.e. earnings, dividends, sales, would suggest and are considered undervalued. Small cap, mid-cap or large cap stocks can also be "value" stocks.

Variable Annuity: A variable annuity is a contract between an investor and an insurance company under which the investor makes a single lump-sum payment or multiple payments in return for a series of periodic payments starting immediately or in the future. The annuity is considered variable because the payments into the contract can be invested in different investment options, and the value of the account may move up or down, depending on the performance of the investment options chosen.

Venture Capital: A type of private equity capital organized to raise capital for start-up companies, or those in the early process of developing products or services.

Yield: The income return on the capital that you've placed in an investment, expressed as a percentage. Bonds provide yield in the form of interest payments and stocks through dividends.

Zero Coupon Bond: A bond that does not pay periodic interest, instead, is sold at a discount and matures at face value. When the bond matures or is called, the investor will receive their initial investment back plus the interest that has accrued. Note that investors must still pay income tax every year on the "phantom" interest that has accrued each year.

About the Author

Arthur Montgomery is a registered representative of and a branch manager for Walnut Street Securities, member FINRA and SIPC. He has been affiliated with Walnut Street Securities since 1992. His branch office is located in Des Peres, Missouri, a lovely little community just outside St. Louis.

Since 1997, Arthur has been married to Patti Montgomery (McDevitt) and they have three wonderful children: Audrey, born in 2000; Stuart, born in 2001; and Lawrence, born in 2007.

Arthur specializes in working with organizations and individuals and their investment management needs. The Walnut Street Securities branch office that Arthur manages oversees the activities of forty-five investment professionals who work with over 13,500 clients.

Arthur's company, Paramount Financial, is an independent financial services firm that was started in 2001. This was established to allow Arthur the flexibility to offer services customized to his clients needs.

Arthur has served on the NASD/FINRA district committee and the FINRA consultative committee. He has served on the Walnut Street Securities Representative Advisory Board and has been involved with many community charities and not-for-profit organizations. He has been listed in the Financial Services who's who list and been awarded the Crescendo's Five Star wealth managers award three years in a row.

The Five Star award is granted by Crescendo, an independent, third-party marketing firm. This award may not represent the experience of all clients and is not indicative of future performance or success. This award stems strictly from client experiences as an insurance or securities product customer.

Branch Office:
11600 Manchester Road, Suite 100, St. Louis, MO 63131
Phone: (314) 238-0207